HERBERT VON KARAJAN

HERBERT
VON KARAJAN
MY AUTOBIOGRAPHY

As told to
Franz Endler

Translated by Stewart Spencer

SIDGWICK & JACKSON
LONDON

First published in Great Britain in 1989 by Sidgwick & Jackson Limited
Originally published in Austria as Herbert von Karajan:
Mein Lebensbericht by J & V Edition Wien Verlagsges. m.b.H.

ISBN 0-283-99723-0

Typeset by Hewer Text Composition Services, Edinburgh

Printed by Mackays of Chatham PLC, Chatham, Kent
for Sidgwick & Jackson Limited
1 Tavistock Chambers, Bloomsbury Way
London WC1A 2SG

Contents

Foreword

The first sentence on the tape transcript of this book reads: 'I can't write about myself, I can only talk about myself.' It was only when I read the complete transcript of our conversations that I realized what a great difference there is between a verbal account of someone's life and a biography set down in written form. Much of it reads differently. Much of it can be captured only approximately.

But isn't every attempt to describe a person an act of interpretation? The interpretation of a human being? There must be an infinite number of ways of distilling a musical experience from a sequence of notes on the written page and thus of acquiring a kind of insight into life. Who can be so presumptuous as to present this work of his as 'uniquely valid'? It says just as much about the notes on the page and the person so described as it does about the conductor or the person expressing his opinion about someone else. And if, as on this occasion, you can help the other person to come to a clearer understanding, then you yourself may also gain from the experience, as I myself did on this occasion.

Herbert von Karajan

Introduction

The 1987 Salzburg Festival opened with a performance in the Grosses Festspielhaus under Herbert von Karajan. Not only was it a different orchestra from the one he had conducted at his own Easter Festival earlier that summer, he also had to take charge, musically and administratively, of a live broadcast of the concert for Austrian television. In addition, he had to rehearse and conduct a major orchestral concert consisting of works by Wagner and, finally, he had to conduct two orchestral concerts with the Berlin Philharmonic, whose guest appearances have now become a traditional part of the Salzburg Festival.

In his capacity as a member of the Festival committee of management, he was invited to attend more frequent and more crucial meetings than had been the case in previous years: more than one 'acute crisis' was dutifully brought to public attention, so that there was the repeated need on the part of the managing committee to react decisively to any problems that suddenly arose. Although it rarely made the headlines, Herbert von Karajan was an active and committed member of the 1987 Salzburg Festival committee of management. Even his attendance at colleagues' rehearsals – those of the producer George Tabori or the conductor Leonard Bernstein, for example – were for him, at least, an accepted part of his duties and workload.

Indirectly connected with the Festival was the opening of a factory which the Japanese firm of Sony had built in Anif just outside Salzburg. Sony were prepared to record his work with the active support of the government and of local industry. Herbert von Karajan had been friendly with Sony's presidents for decades and it was quite clearly he who had attracted the firm to Anif.

He attended the opening ceremony and said a few kind words, ensuring more general interest not so much in himself but in the region's new employer.

Is there need to mention that among the important visitors who came to Salzburg for the Summer Festival, many let it be known that they were keen to have a brief word with Herbert von Karajan, and that the conductor could not spend his whole time avoiding such people? And surely it goes without saying that he himself held meetings of every description with managers, producers, stage designers and also with other conductors?

If Herbert von Karajan were to have his way, the activities of these six brief summer weeks would not be mentioned at all.

But the conductor carried out all these duties under the intense and indiscreet scrutiny of the world's media, which meant that each time he appeared in public he had to put up with the greater part of the Festival's music lovers and almost all professional Karajan watchers attempting, with greater or lesser success, to find out more about the state of his health. For years Herbert von Karajan has borne the reproach of being more than, or other than, a mere musician, and the summer of 1987 was no different in this respect: he was never observed, applauded or criticized as a musician, but was always described according to non-artistic criteria.

Why am I noting all of this down?

Because Herbert von Karajan is the subject of more than one biography to date whose attempts to interpret his life and character he heartily detests, and because the life he led in Salzburg that summer is an extreme example of what is commonly reported about him. Because, in his work and daily contacts, he gave the lie to most of the stories that are spread about him. And because he did so secretly, as it were, not even hinting that he may have deserved to be treated differently.

To be treated differently?

It is the aim of the present book, part biography, part auto-biography, to accord him the treatment he properly deserves. It is, I hope, a record of the eightieth year of the conductor's life.

'Basically, I can only talk about my life,' was the first sentence of a voluminous manuscript written solely on the basis of tape transcripts of the detailed conversations which took place between us, transcripts which were then typed up and submitted to him for approval.

'One day I'd like to find time to write a book about a number of general musical questions – there are already handwritten notes, but they're far from complete, and it's an effort for me to find the definitive way of expressing myself. I shall have to spend a long time on this book, assuming I'm granted the time to do so. But I'll never be able to write a proper autobiography. That's something I can only talk about.'

With these words Herbert von Karajan began an attempt to answer all manner of inquisitive and indiscreet questions, and to express his opinion on other topics that he may have preferred not to be put to him, in other words, to dictate a 'proper autobiography'. He spent three years on this project, attending many sessions, giving many interviews and offering many extremely new points of view. When I then showed him what he himself had said, his reaction was again one of dissatisfaction. 'I know that's what I said. But I know I would never have written it. It's the same problem as when I started. I can't write about my life, I can't even talk about it, I can only give you information.'

The following pages are a reaction to what, provisionally, is Herbert von Karajan's final word on the subject of autobiography. They are an extended interview given over a period of more than three years. Responsibility for the questions that were asked and for the subjects that were scarcely touched on no longer rests solely with Herbert von Karajan but also extends to his interviewer – I was simply not able to formulate many of the questions I would otherwise have asked. But Karajan himself encouraged me to include not only actual quotations from our conversations but also to take account of his marginal observations and treat them as part of the interview.

But there was another obligation which I accepted and which neither frivolousness nor the thought of financial gain would prevent me from keeping. According to our agreement, Herbert von Karajan would have the opportunity to read through the

3

whole text and to accept or reject it. No book would appear without his express approval.

In a few months' time what is called, somewhat euphemistically, the musical world will be celebrating Herbert von Karajan's eightieth birthday. Book and interview are intended as a birthday tribute to him. But if I understand the matter aright, they will be Herbert von Karajan's gift to the musical world.

Franz Endler
1988

Childhood in Salzburg

Herbert von Karajan's admirers have always been starved of real information concerning the conductor's life, surroundings and habits. In the past they could cut out pictures of Karajan on board his yacht or at the controls of his private jet, and use these photographs to build up an imaginary picture of all the other aspects of his life. But in recent years even these pictures have disappeared from the pages of glossy magazines. The only glimpse the general public now gets of Herbert von Karajan is as a conductor or a producer. Always anxious to keep his distance, Karajan has done everything possible to ensure that his life should be even quieter and less sensational than ever.

Even in Salzburg where he came into the world, where he conducted his first orchestral concert and where, after the Second World War, he made a fresh start, finally establishing his own Festival with its final chord extending over many decades, it is difficult to know whether he is in town or not when he is hard at work.

Whenever I play back the conversations which I had with Herbert von Karajan, I have the distinct impression, even after more than two years of so-called contact with him, that he not only approves of the absolute secrecy that surrounds his private life, but is happy that it should be so. It may be that in the past he intentionally kept reporters at bay, even though he knew how many legends were bound to arise when a famous conductor like himself failed to satisfy an inquisitive world. It is certainly the case now that, at the age of eighty, he is happy to be left alone to concentrate on his day's work and not to suffer outside interference.

Where Karajan lives and works there must be peace and

quiet. Around him are all the necessary technical aids which he uses to listen to music, to dictate messages and to make telephone calls. He refuses to say anything about the 'style' of the rooms in which he is at home. He is careful to cut off his private sphere of existence from public gaze. He will not even allow people to write about the extremely plain rooms in which he works. Any such suggestion is dismissed with a single word. For Karajan it goes without saying that his surroundings must be perfectly quiet, and that they no doubt are when he sits in front of monitors, editing music films or checking tapes that have already been edited.

He does not explain this in so many words, but he agrees with my own explanation that he releases his energy only at the opportune moment, and that he therefore regards loud sentences and extravagant gestures as a waste of that energy, intentionally avoiding all encounters which will demand too much emotional effort of him. With his closest colleagues he can work efficiently and concentratedly, occasionally catching them off their guard with an eccentrically humorous remark. When he can't avoid visitors, he treats them with the reserved politeness of a self-assured gentleman. It is only in his dealings with musicians and technicians that he appears almost relaxed, treating them as colleagues, allowing himself to reminisce and showing that he is naturally conversant with up-to-the-minute professional gossip. And, if need be, he can also play the part of a grouchy old man who is impossible to please, but he will only do so in order to defuse a tense situation that has built up around an artistic problem.

He knows that his public is curious to know about his family life. But he is not in the least inclined to satisfy such curiosity. In all the conversations which he recorded as part of the present biography, what he had to say about his family would fit on a single sheet of paper. It might have been possible to coax the odd half sentence out of him – but, as someone with candid and detailed views on other topics, Karajan preferred to go back to talking about Furtwängler, Max Reinhardt and the Salzburg Festival.

Because Herbert von Karajan is a well-known personality,

6

constantly in the public eye, many writers feel that he has no right to discretion in the private sphere. I do not share this view. That I did not attempt to question him about his family and discover anything 'new' is something for which I accept full responsibility. I still consider it bad manners to question a person about something when he clearly does not wish to say anything on the subject. And I think it is impertinent to draw particular conclusions from his silence.

There has been far too much speculation in the past as to the reasons why Herbert von Karajan has never given a detailed account of his childhood. I should like to add another one, and one, moreover, which has not been voiced so far. The conductor has been asked far too often in the course of his career about his parental home, his origins and his ancestors. But he himself forgot all about such matters long ago and no longer concerns himself with them. He is not the sort of man to guard sentimental memories or to harbour feelings of resentment. That is why he speaks so sparingly about his family and his childhood.

It seems inexplicable to him today that his mother should have wanted him to go into banking. She rarely figures in the terse accounts he gives of his parental home, but her desire to see him take up banking was evidently so utterly absurd as to remain forever in his memory and even now to cause him to shake his head. That she ran the household and brought up her two sons, as was expected at that time, goes without saying. But that she did not have the same amount of influence on their education as her husband is equally self-evident. Whatever we may know now about the emancipation of women in the years around 1900, word had not yet spread on the subject. In the Karajan household it was their father who was the determining influence.

'It was in my parents' house that I first discovered how music is made. I was still a child when I discovered that music can be made in very different ways.'

Enough has been written about Herbert von Karajan's ambition to keep up with his elder brother Wolfgang's piano lessons, but he himself prefers to remember that he sang in the local choir. 'Choral singing has in fact accompanied me throughout my life,' he says and unexpectedly draws a vast unifying curve

7

over his hitherto unknown involvement in various church choirs in Salzburg, his first encounters with professional choruses at the Salzburg Festival, his work as chorus master in the smaller theatres where he was engaged, and his encounter with the Vienna Singverein, which elected him their concert director for life in 1949.

His evident attempt to interpret his life in terms of continuity succeeds astonishingly well in the field of choral singing. 'When I finally had the Vienna chorus at my disposal, I knew that here was the ideal instrument for my tonal visions. Together with the Singverein, which, after all, embodies a most venerable tradition (it was they who brought Johannes Brahms to Vienna in the nineteenth century), I have not only rehearsed concerts, I have also built up a repertory over the decades, renewing and perfecting it through countless rehearsals. With the Singverein it has basically never been a question of working for a concert but always of rehearsing for later concerts. And it was only logical that we should later go on tour together, not only making recordings and films of the great choral works but giving concerts throughout the world. Today the Singverein is like an extension of my own arm. We understand each other all the time. We don't need to discuss things. We know that we'll never stop making music together.'

Karajan himself never alludes to those events which, at the time, seemed world-shaking in their importance. Yet he admits that not only the members of the chorus itself but also the Gesellschaft der Musikfreunde in general recall the times when, even though his links with Vienna were seriously disrupted, he none the less remained in contact with the city, above all on a musical level. There has not been a period when he has not conducted the Vienna Philharmonic and the Singverein of the Gesellschaft der Musikfreunde. These two institutions, which he heard as a child and which he learned to prize as a young man, have every reason to be proud of his loyalty. And his passion for choral singing could easily be attested by recalling the various musical performances he has conducted.

All too rarely has this been attempted in the past. Karajan himself has only just mentioned it now. When he looks back on his childhood and adolescence, what is important is no longer the piano prodigy that he was for a brief period, but his membership of the various church choirs in which he sang as a child.

At the same time, it has to be said that Herbert von Karajan's singing voice, so often heard at rehearsals and sometimes even at performances, is scarcely noted for its melodious qualities. He is famed for giving his singers safer and more encouraging support than any other conductor; he knows everything about voices, but although he might want to sing himself, he cannot in fact do so. He makes others sing, in every sense of the word.

His remark that it was while he was still at home that he discovered in how many different ways music can be made does not of course refer to choral singing. His father, the leading doctor at Salzburg's regional hospital and a passionate musician, played the piano and clarinet. In the latter capacity he was often prevailed upon to play in the Mozarteum Orchestra, which gave regular performances in the Salzburg Landestheater.

'I can remember not only the music that we played at home, I can also remember exactly what the orchestra of my childhood sounded like. And I know that there isn't a music lover alive today who would be able to put up with the concerts it gave. We came together for a single rehearsal for each concert, and the works that were on the programme were played through once. And immediately afterwards came the public concert.' For Herbert von Karajan there is a remark which he associates with orchestral musicians and which he still remembers from his childhood days in Salzburg: 'We've got the piece off pat'.

Whenever he repeats this sentence and recalls how often he has heard it in his life, he shudders visibly and is of the opinion that, although times have changed and the level of orchestral playing has everywhere reached an incomparably higher standard, the mentality of the musicians he knew as a child still exists. 'As far as preparing for a concert or opera performance was concerned, most of the famous great ensembles of my childhood were no different from what it was like in Salzburg. I know, because I was often in Vienna and heard the best musicians of the time there. But basically everything sounded very, very under-rehearsed. This ghastly sentence was repeated even by the Vienna Philharmonic after a quick run-through of a piece they barely knew.'

Nonetheless, it was because of this liberal relationship of musicians towards rehearsals and the passionate enthusiasm of amateur players that Karajan was able to hear such a large repertoire during his childhood years in the small town of Salzburg. 'My parents' house was a meeting-place for all the town's musicians; my father took me along with him to his orchestra rehearsals. I remember this much better than I do the early years spent studying the piano and performing in public. People called me a child prodigy, but it was never my intention to be a child prodigy.'

Herbert von Karajan trivializes the many reports of his public appearances in Salzburg. He may have been a child prodigy, a budding pianist. But he did not become a pianist, and so his earliest attempts to do so are as good as forgotten. They are of no interest to him. And they are certainly not overshadowed by any 'rivalry' with his brother Wolfgang, who had begun having piano lessons before him and who, as an organist, was to give regular concerts throughout his life.

'My brother was simply my elder brother. He began to have music lessons before I did and became interested in technology before I did. But there came a time when we started to develop in completely separate directions, and for years we had practically nothing to do with each other.' Karajan does not talk about his brother, who died in 1987, but passes straight from him to the subject of Bach, speaking enthusiastically and at length about Glenn Gould, whose recordings of *The Art of Fugue* he considers a model of their kind and whose lifestyle and way of performing he praises to the skies.

'What a pianist, what a musician Glenn Gould was! If you listen closely to his recordings, you can sense all that. His way of finding the right speed. His handling of the instrument. His understanding of Bach's architecture. I always understood why he wanted to withdraw from public performances and have his own recording studio, and why he made music exactly as he himself wanted to. A pianist with his abilities could not survive in any other way. I often thought of working with him one day. His death was a great loss to the world.'

Karajan was a child of Salzburg, but one with abundant musical experience. This he gained in Vienna.

'My uncle was technical director of the state theatres. In other words, he was responsible for all theatre buildings. What that meant for us was that we could always use his free seats at the opera whenever we were in Vienna. And we kept on returning to Vienna. I grew up in a small town. But even at that time I knew exactly how music was performed in Vienna at the Opera and the Musikverein. And it did not take long to realize that Vienna was of course the Mecca for us musicians, but that we would not hear ideal performances or concerts every evening.'

For Karajan, who is not especially interested in the history of music, it goes without saying that musical performances throughout the nineteenth century were slovenly in the extreme; famous exceptions such as the Meiningen Orchestra really *were* exceptions; and what is now taken for granted in matters of precision playing did not come into fashion until long after the turn of the century. He lived in Salzburg, grew up during the early years of the Salzburg Festival, and was present when the first rehearsal fanatics began to work in Salzburg – the producer Max Reinhardt and, somewhat later, the conductor Arturo Toscanini. And at the same time he was already involved in the Festival to the extent that he could not only see exactly how it was run but judge its organization with a degree of competence which enables him to say that basically little has changed there during the last fifty or sixty years.

'I was involved in the Festival from the very beginning. I was in the boys' choir, then one of the stage extras, and then a young music student who was allowed to stand in the wings and cue in the chorus or the onstage musicians. In other words, I have known from childhood onwards what musical quality really means.' And almost without a transition, 'Incidentally, the Salzburg Festival always depended even then on one or two leading figures. I know Arturo Toscanini is said to have thrown a fit when it was suggested that Wilhelm Furtwängler should be engaged. Toscanini declared that the Salzburg Festival was

11

his season, and he dictated which operas he wanted to conduct. There was never any discussion. The operas he wanted to conduct were scheduled for the times when he wanted to conduct them. But Bruno Walter was basically just the same. He came and declared in his much more conciliatory manner that he would conduct *Oberon*, whether this was acceptable in Salzburg or not. And of course he had to have his way, and arrangements had to be made for the performances which, quietly but firmly, he insisted on giving. This sort of thing was rarely discussed in my youth, and virtually nothing was said or written about such matters in public. But, of course, the Festival was run in the way that Reinhardt or Walter or Toscanini wanted. And everyone was happy to be able to attend their performances. And I was overjoyed at the possibility of attending all their rehearsals and, at the same time, learning these operas by heart.'

The function of the Salzburg Festival, which even today provokes leading articles and inflames politicians, has altered just as little. The changes which the town underwent following the institutionalization of the Festival can still be seen, and, as always, are commented on in ways that are not always entirely positive. The Festival as an economic factor, as a way of attracting tourism, as an important prop in the country's attempt to remind the world that Austria is the land of music: this was how the young Herbert von Karajan got to know it as a child, and that is how he still sees it today. And that is how he would define it in the future, if he did not have other, reassuringly humorous remarks to make about Salzburg, as will emerge much later.

The existence of the Festival, the status which music enjoyed in the small town, the self-evident delight in music which he felt in his parents' house – these were factors which make the young Herbert von Karajan's choice of a career more understandable. He wanted to be a musician, a pianist.

'My father said, "I know you have a gift for music. But you ought at least to try your hand at some practical profession." That's what was said at the time, and it sounded fairly plausible. I was used to listening to my father, and so I went to Vienna to study technology. For me, it was a kind of attempt to please him. But I was genuinely interested in every kind of technology and have never lost that interest. The fascination which I feel for a new design or a technologically plausible piece is something I have retained to this day. Even though I very soon gave up my studies in Vienna, I am still technically minded in my own way. I have always tried to keep up-to-date concerning new discoveries and ideas; and I still subscribe to a number of specialist journals.'

The world knows how publicly Herbert von Karajan has proclaimed his interest in technological progress, and the world of music knows how often this interest has been interpreted negatively. The image of the musician, remote from all gadgets and technological aids and communing alone with the composer, is a more popular one but, at the same time, less intelligent than the vision of an interpreter who ensures that he has not only the latest instruments but also the best technological support in order to realize his musical ideas.

In spite of their conscientious search for all the relevant documents, previous biographers have never been able to establish the exact number of terms that Herbert von Karajan studied technology in Vienna. No doubt the conductor himself has been less than communicative in this respect; in all conversations on the subject he behaves very much as though he had little interest in providing precise dates or quotable documents. And the woman he mentions in passing as having built up a Karajan archive also has little to say. She, too, enjoys less than the full co-operation of the maestro, who, although he is generally believed to be working away every day on his own 'legend', in fact does little to prevent the dispersal and disappearance of information which, taken together, might make up that legend.

Where other artists employ solicitous housewives or loyal fans to gather statistics and collect reviews, Karajan behaves in a wholly disinterested manner. He does not have a single important date in his head, never knows exactly how long he has been working with an orchestra or with any top-ranking institution, and would be incapable of celebrating all the anniversaries which naturally befall a man of his age. He is only proud of the fact that, according to the statistics, he has cancelled scarcely more than one per cent of all his contractual obligations. It needs an orchestra or some other organization to come along, open its archives and draw Herr von Karajan's attention to the fact that an anniversary is imminent. And even when that has been achieved, the institution in question is still far from certain that Herr von Karajan will appear.

'I never again moved away from music during my time in Vienna. I was preparing for a career as a pianist. I studied with Josef Hoffmann and had all the musical abilities necessary to become a pianist. But then I had a bad attack of neuritis, I had problems with the sinews between my index finger and middle finger, and I tried the most absurd remedies. I prepared dressings and supports and would rather have regarded my hands as permanently damaged than have given up. I simply refused to pay attention to my illness.' His teachers showed him a way out of the crisis. What teachers? There is a letter written decades later in which Herbert von Karajan expressly thanks Bernhard Paumgartner for pointing him in the direction of conducting. But there are also the notes which I made on the basis of my conversations with Karajan, in which he expressly states (again many years after the events in question) that it was not Paumgartner but his teacher in Vienna who advised him to enrol on the conducting course. Perhaps, exceptionally, I might be allowed to decide between these two versions. In the light of conversations with his old Salzburg teacher and family friend, Bernhard Paumgartner, and on the advice of his Viennese mentor, whom he expressly described as a good teacher, Karajan himself decided to embark on a conducting career. The justification ('What do you hope to achieve with the piano? I am convinced that chamber music cannot give you what an orchestra has in store for you') sounds so much like Karajan himself that one can claim with a clear conscience that it was he himself who first had the idea.

'And so I became a student in the conducting class at the Vienna Academy. I should add, however, that Clemens Krauss was no longer in Vienna, no other conductor had been found to succeed him, and the class was taught by Alexander Wunderer. He was a member of the Vienna Philharmonic, an outstanding musician, and later joined the orchestra's board of management.

14

But as a teacher there was of course little he could do apart from teaching us what are called the tools of the profession. In other words, I learned my trade, like the rest of the students in my year, through self-help.' Self-help?

'We were a kind of club. We were for ever at the Opera, where we stood at the back of the gallery, watching the conductor. The parents of one of my colleagues were well-off and owned two pianos, so we simply went off to his place and played through all the works that were then in the repertory at the opera house. Two of us played the piano, another sang the solo parts, a fourth the chorus and a fifth conducted. And when we had worked through the whole of an opera in this way, we went back to the Opera, listened to the performance and then went for a drink, complaining to a man about the inferior quality of what we had just heard.'

For those of us who are familiar with the apparently unsociable, reserved conductor that Karajan now is, such an account is difficult to credit, but it must be true, since Karajan literally blossoms at this point in the conversation as he talks about this kind of auto-instruction, of the afternoons spent at the piano, the evenings in the amphitheatre at the Opera and the lively discussions that went on till late into the night. 'I am still convinced that this is the best way of experiencing music. And I know that we learned something then that could never again be taken away from us. Such things are no longer available today. Nowadays the careers of young conductors are differently mapped out. They have to be quicker, more superficial, almost as a matter of necessity.'

If one listens closely, it is not the young musicians whom Karajan blames. He simply observes what conditions are like nowadays and maintains that it is therefore no longer possible to learn the profession in the way that he himself did.

Does Herbert von Karajan have pupils? In the strict sense of the word, no, since, with the exception of a handful of courses, he has never taught. But he himself is of the view that he does have pupils. On the one hand there are the many conductors who have now risen to prominence and whom he helped at the beginning of their careers by talking to them as colleagues for hours on end, helping them to solve problems in a score or giving them advice. And there are also internationally acknowledged conductors, such as Seiji Ozawa, whom he regards as his pupils since he allowed them to attend his rehearsals, often for months on end. 'I always told them, I cannot teach you how to conduct. I can only show you how to rehearse an orchestra. And rehearse them, moreover, in such a way that you scarcely need to conduct them at the concert afterwards.' There are many conductors, therefore, who can describe themselves as Karajan's pupils; indeed, a number of extremely distinguished conductors would have to admit to being classified as such.

He blames the time and a number of institutions, quoting Sir Thomas Beecham, who once said of him, 'Any fool can conduct four programmes', and expressing regret that it is now possible to tour the world 'with a very narrow repertory'. He remembers the time he stayed in New York and saw a young conductor clearly conducting a work for the first time at the Met. In answer to Karajan's question whether such a thing was really possible, the general manager Rudolf Bing told him, 'Well, he has to learn somewhere'.

The realist none the less comes to terms with reality, and Karajan is not the man to look on the black side of things. There are young conductors, as he himself repeatedly discovers, whom he regards as highly gifted.

'When the time came for my first public appearance at an Academy concert during my period of study in Vienna, I knew exactly what I wanted. The programme consisted mainly of arias and duets, and all we had to do was accompany. I banked everything on being able to conduct the only work that was actually intended for the orchestra – it was the overture to Rossini's *William Tell*. The rehearsals were held in the presence of the entire professorial staff, Franz Schmidt was the principal and took the chair. Those of my fellow students who had preceded me had gone through their paces and shown themselves to be as effective as was possible in the circumstances. Then I came and worked with the orchestra. We were expected simply to conduct the overture straight through, but even at that stage I was already saying things like, "Each trumpet on its own, please" and "No,

16

there is no rhythm to what you are playing". I worked in this way for about ten minutes on the first terse entry of the trumpets. Franz Schmidt then stood up and announced that the test was over. "I believe, gentlemen, that we now know enough," he said to the other professors.' And Karajan, as he himself now says, had found his style, a style with which he has repeatedly sought to convince clever orchestral musicians and fascinated observers. 'At the concert itself I conducted very calmly and without any strain. After all, we had rehearsed.'

And that is all that Herbert von Karajan has to say about his student days in Vienna. Of course, he enthuses about the city's musical life and about the musicians he heard in his youth, and he remembers the concerts given by leading pianists. And when he takes the rare opportunity to think aloud about the state of some opera house or other, it is clear that he still remembers details from his youth.

'You must not forget what Vienna's Golden Age was really like. There were the great names that we still remember today, but they liked to cancel, and then one or other of the local tenors would be waiting in the wings to be called out on stage as a substitute. I know that people still enthuse about Slezak, Piccaver and Schmedes today. But most evenings it was Josef Kahlenberg who sang. And quite respectably, too.'

A similar thought occurs to Karajan when the chance arises to reminisce about the Gesellschaft der Musikfreunde between the wars. 'For us the Great Hall was the hall of the gods. When I came to Vienna, I thought I'd hear only the very best concerts. But I had a good enough ear to realize that even the Vienna Philharmonic gave bad concerts. It could not be otherwise. Neither in the concert hall nor in the opera house is it possible or desirable to have one high point after another. Audiences would not be able to tolerate it in the long term.'

Herbert von Karajan has no recollection of any experiences in Vienna unconnected with his music studies or with the opera performances and concerts that he attended. So he gives further proof of his unprecedentedly selective memory which sifts through all his experiences and throws out whatever is of no use.

17

So, too, he demonstrates his resolve not to alter anything even if it were to benefit his image to do so.

Karajan's ancestors were prominent figures in imperial Vienna and were distinguished for their personal merit and for their achievements. Herbert von Karajan never speaks of them. He collects neither souvenirs nor paintings, and prefers to leave those paintings which his admirers have bought for him in the offices of the Gesellschaft der Musikfreunde in Vienna. In conversation, the only member of his family who is important to him is his uncle, who regularly obtained tickets for him at the Opera. In response to intense questioning, it occurs to him that his mother wanted him to go into banking, and that his father wanted him to gain professional qualifications. He and his brother (who was also studying in Vienna) went their separate ways. It was an unemotional parting. Karajan's goal was music.

'When I finished my studies, I wanted to know more details. I wanted to find out whether I could conduct a concert, what I could achieve with a professional orchestra. Although it was clear to me that I could not begin a career in my home town, I hired the Mozarteum Orchestra for an evening. My father and all our family friends helped to advertise the concert. As a former child prodigy I had a certain prestige – but this and the favourable notices I had received as a child would not have been enough on their own. Outside the Festival season Salzburg was still a small, very sleepy town.' The concert took place in January 1929. On the programme were Tchaikovsky's Fifth Symphony, Mozart's A major Piano Concerto K488, and Richard Strauss's *Don Juan*.

In describing not only this first concert but all subsequent events of any importance, Herbert von Karajan always seems to speak of them as successfully fought battles. And he describes the negotiations surrounding these concerts and opera performances as though they had all progressed along similar lines: there was always a great deal of good luck, always a great willingness on Karajan's part to take risks, and always wearying delays in the course of getting things done.

'The concert was a great success. I had good reviews. But most important of all, the intendant of the Ulm Stadttheater was in the audience, and afterwards invited me to Ulm for a trial performance. I told him, "It's pointless. I'll come at once if you'll give me the chance to conduct a new production. At the end of a week you can tell me if you don't like me. And I'll go away again with no hard feelings. But I myself would like to rehearse the work that you want me to conduct." '

Early Career in Ulm

Herbert von Karajan's debut in Ulm took place almost immediately after his concert in Salzburg and the above conversation with his first intendant.

Following a suitable rehearsal period he conducted *The Marriage of Figaro* on 2 March 1929: it was the first time he had conducted an opera in his life, and the theatre management responded by offering him a contract for the 1929/30 season. He was an opera conductor in a small town and had to share the work with a colleague. It was a provincial appointment.

'It is almost impossible today to imagine how small and primitive our theatre was. The proscenium arch was six metres wide. The whole stage was no bigger than a decent-sized living room. The chorus was small, the orchestra had thirty-two players in it and could be enlarged only in exceptional cases. The repertory could never be played for any length of time. We had to present one première after another.'

Thus Karajan reminisces in the shadow of the Grosses Festspielhaus. There is certainly no sense of false nostalgia to his account of the conditions under which he began his career. But nor does he grow despondent about a way of performing plays and operas which has always been totally alien to him. He simply states what things were like in 1929 and under what conditions he performed and learned his trade over a period of many years.

'I never had time to worry unduly. My work in Ulm was not limited to conducting performances. As répétiteur I had to work through new roles with singers who were not exactly distinguished, we were in charge of chorus rehearsals, we had to prepare for first nights which, in turn, had to be rehearsed

21

in quick succession, while in between times the company went on tour, performing operettas in the surrounding towns and villages. The orchestra was much too small, and, of course, it was more than weak: the instruments which we did not have at our disposal were always improvised on the piano. It would have been sheer torment to play a proper score with this orchestra, but there was no time to think of any kind of torment. I kept myself going by completely different means. I always had the music in my head as it was supposed to sound. And I simply closed my ears in despair at what we were actually producing. At that time I would keep on repeating to myself, "Study, study, and don't say a word about what you can hear and see. Simply shut your mouth and get on with your work." I find that is the only attitude to adopt and the only way of really learning to master your profession. When my daughter joined the theatre some time ago and was struggling with the tiniest roles and with all the difficulties that beginners have to face, I gave her the one piece of advice that I had given myself almost sixty years previously, "Shut your mouth and study, and get on with your work!"

'There were two conductors in Ulm – my colleague was called Otto Schulmann, his father owned a small private bank in Munich. Of course, the system was planned in such a way that each conductor took his own rehearsals and conducted all later performances himself. But we could make our own arrangements, and the intendant, who noticed what we wanted, placed few obstacles in our way. Sometimes one of us would fall ill, and the other of us might find himself conducting an opera which was not yet in his repertory. In this way I came across some forty operas during my time in Ulm which I know I could take over and conduct today with only a day's preparation. And, if you are honest with yourself, these forty operas are basically today's entire operatic repertory. Of course, we also performed works in Ulm which are no longer given. And, of course, there are other novelties which find their way into the repertory today. But if you exclude all of these and consider what an opera house needs to get by – both then and now – then you come down to thirty or, at most, forty works which are the ones performed in every theatre.'

The world of opera, in which Herbert von Karajan is regarded not only as a magus and magnet, but also as its undisputed and most senior professional, does not, as a general rule, consist of scholars. It is preoccupied with concerns other than the enormous number of works that have been performed only once, and it rarely thinks about the minimum number of really popular pieces. Even after a long and successful life in opera, Herbert von Karajan is not prepared to theorize. He is a practising musician who notes what the reality of the situation is – an artistic genre which, under certain conditions, can hold the world in suspense and whose attractiveness is based not on thousands of works but on the forty operas to which he has referred. He still knows them all by heart and claims that in an emergency he would still be able to conduct them, having got to know them at the beginning of his career in Ulm, working with individual singers, taking rehearsals and conducting performances of them during eight hard years of provincial employment under conditions so primitive that it is difficult nowadays to imagine what it must really have been like.

And this was at a time when politics was an essential and integral part of people's lives. Even today Karajan is not above attack, but at least he is now prepared to raise the issue himself. Yet he does so in his own way, ignoring all the existing documents and records, and describing the situation as he himself recalls it. 'One of my conducting colleagues was Jewish. And an enthusiastic supporter of the National Socialist movement. We got along famously together, working harmoniously and yet always finding time to discuss current affairs. It astonished me to discover how much interest he took in what was going on, and how passionately he spoke out in favour of something that ought really to have been no business of his. I remember his coming to see me one day, immediately after the election results had been announced, and saying, "We've won. I'll have to say goodbye now, there's nothing else for me to do here in Germany." As a politically minded person, he was satisfied with the outcome. He was proud of the fact that all his predictions had come true and that even the list of ministers which he had drawn up in his head had proved to be correct. But it was equally clear to him that he would have to leave his beloved Germany. We have never lost sight of each other completely, and I'm still in correspondence with him. He lives in Los Angeles.'

And, as before, Karajan never comes back to the working conditions or the living conditions in Ulm, nor to this entire chapter in his life. Now and again he mentions, for example, that his work as répétiteur with singers of less than the first rank has made it possible for him to react correctly to potential problems suffered by today's leading singers. On one occasion he even gives a demonstration of his working methods, not in Ulm in 1930, but in Salzburg in 1986. He has just attended two detailed lighting rehearsals for *Don Carlos*. He returns to his room in the Grosses Festspielhaus, sits down at the piano with the young Italian soprano Fiamma Izzo d'Amico, and goes through her part with her for two hours. He rehearses the role of Elisabeth with her, unyieldingly, singing all her partners' cues and not only giving her all her entries but, above all, encouraging her to feel that she is capable of bringing off the most difficult passages. Time and again he tells her in Italian, English and German, 'You don't have to prove to anyone that you have a big voice. What you have to show me is that you can sing a well-supported *pianissimo* above the stave. We shall be quiet enough to support you. The *pianissimo* is difficult. But if you cannot manage it, you are just an ordinary soprano from Italy.'

It is regrettable, but no doubt it cannot be helped. In the tiny, sparsely furnished rehearsal room, where anything other than the piano and a couple of chairs would be out of place, it has so far proved impossible to capture the intensity with which Herbert von Karajan works with his singers. There are private tape recordings which the singers themselves make in order to be able to practise on their own at a later date, and perhaps they even keep them as private souvenirs. But Karajan's rasping voice, as he sings passages from an opera, performing Posa or Carlos or King Philip and at the same time, or almost at the same time, encouraging his Elisabeth to repeat a particular passage and find the right *pianissimo* – this voice has not been recorded for Karajan's admirers. It belongs solely and uniquely to the singers and musicians who work with

24

him. To them he is a well-qualified and fascinating helper. But only to them.

Another opportunity presents itself to raise the question of Herbert von Karajan's time in Ulm. He has made the necessary sound recordings for the 1987 New Year's Day concert and has sent for a copy of one of the tapes to listen to. In one of the overtures the orchestra deviates minimally from Johann Strauss, and the conductor is more disconsolate than I have ever seen him before. He feels that he should have heard it and that it should never have been allowed to happen. Not to a person like himself, who had struck up an immediate rapport with Johann Strauss and the Vienna Philharmonic from the very first rehearsal.

'I don't know what to say about my affinity with this music. Johann Strauss – he's someone, after all, whom we have all grown up with, there are as good as no discussions about tempi or about any other musical questions. And as for operetta, the way we performed these works in Ulm has left its mark on me. That was an experience to last a lifetime. Improvisation was, so to speak, inevitable. Maybe it is no longer possible to imagine how we performed these operas. But when you look at the operetta theatres that still exist, you may perhaps get an idea of how we performed operettas at that time.'

Not even Karajan's most industrious biographers have yet discovered any documents relating to his earliest public appearance conducting an operetta, and some of them dispute whether he and the Ulm company ever undertook sorties into even more remote provincial fastnesses. For me, there are no such doubts. It seems to me inconceivable that a conducter who was engaged in Ulm could have absented himself from duty, or that an Austrian conductor trained in Vienna should have been passed over in this way. And the fact that Herbert von Karajan knows what he is talking about when describing, with something approaching a smile, the manner in which these operettas were performed puts paid to any lingering doubts.

Herbert von Karajan has given me his express permission to flesh out those parts of his portrait which he himself cannot be bothered to complete. In other words, he has encouraged me – a journalist for years regarded as his most outspoken adversary by those members of the general public who are interested in festivals and music generally – to attempt to reproduce his impressions on the basis of our many conversations, conversations which have been extremely difficult and emotionally very taxing. If this challenge is to be faced, it must be faced now, not at the end of this book.

I have known Herbert von Karajan since childhood – at least insofar as anyone can claim to know another person. At that time I saw him and watched him rehearsing and performing at the Musikverein, and the impression I formed then was of an uncompromising musician who expected the utmost degree of concentration from all his fellow artists over alarmingly long periods. And who never, never raised his voice or was rude to others.

Later, at what was described as the pinnacle of his power, I was able to observe him from close quarters. He was (amongst other things) artistic director of the Vienna State Opera. His attitude towards the general public, but also towards critics, was one of glacial politeness and great reserve. But he could not prevent people from sensing that he had some difficulty in establishing human contact with his closest colleagues, and he was certainly misunderstood when he was said to have raised himself to a position of lofty isolation. During the days and months when he appeared to be floating in the clouds and not deigning to negotiate with subordinate officials or with government ministries, he was extremely human and normal when dealing with musicians, stage staff or other sympathetic experts inside his own opera house.

And when, with the help of a few effective remarks, he reduced his links with musical Vienna to a barely perceptible minimum and was available only briefly for comment in the VIP lounge at Vienna's Schwechat airport, the general public continued to think of him as a great non-communicator. Yet he suddenly began to talk freely to a number of journalists, chatting about the undesirable side effects of a particular brand of cigarettes or asking about the most recent concerts in Vienna. I shall not forget this conversation, not least because it was on this occasion that he learned of Claudio Abbado's earliest successes, as a direct result of which Abbado was invited to Salzburg.

26

Now, decades later, Abbado is jointly responsible for running the Vienna State Opera.

Once again, decades have gone by. Herbert von Karajan has realized his dream of perfection with his own Easter Festival and has not only revised his views on the possible private financing of the Festival but adapted those views to suit prevailing conditions. Above all, however, he has a number of serious operations behind him which have left him severely handicapped. Karajan himself refused to talk about this for as long as was possible and thus tried to hide the truth from himself. He finally had a support built for himself on the podium in front of his orchestra only when it became impossible for him to conduct a whole concert standing. He has given up practically all the different kinds of sport which he used to enjoy and has directed his energies instead to those areas of his life's work that he plans to leave behind him.

And he has tried on many occasions, in conversation with writers, to clarify his thoughts and his current views on both the past and the present. If I may be allowed to interpret the facts at this point, it seems to me that he has tended to turn to interested parties who are only partially familiar with music, and that he has always avoided anyone from Vienna. He has previously had difficulties when describing, however allusively, what a long-standing music lover from Vienna understands straightaway. His incomplete sentences were misunderstood, and his desire to avoid some topic or other, or to discuss it expressly from his own very personal point of view, was not respected.

It may come as something of a surprise therefore that, notwithstanding these disappointments, he has now invited someone to talk to him who for many years was described in public as his 'opponent'. But that is what has happened. And Karajan's sentences, encapsulated on tape, are expressly his, even if they sometimes have to be slightly recast for the printed page. At all events, they definitely reveal what he wants to say. Although he is now in his eightieth year, he speaks neither hesitatingly nor unintelligibly. If he appears not to hear a question, it is because he does not want to hear it. If he keeps on pushing aside memories of his long life and returning to what he is currently working on

27

and what he wants to finish, his manner is neither impatient nor insistent, he is simply on the ball.

Amusing? Even now, Herbert von Karajan does not seem especially so. And yet, like any other Austrian musician recalling the events of his past life, he remembers witty and trenchant remarks which he claims to have heard or to have said himself. And, of course, like every other artist, he knows a host of anecdotes about his predecessors or rivals, and there is a certain mastery about the way he tells these stories. But a tape transcript is not the right way to record these remarks of Karajan's, since some of the stories end in outstretched arms, others in a shrug of the shoulders, but most of all they end in a facial expression that says more than words ever could. And you always have to ask yourself whether, as he talks away uninhibitedly, your opposite number intends what he is saying to be recorded. He does not consider it necessary to point out that this or that was said in confidence. I think he considers it a waste of time to keep on showing consideration in this way during a collaborative venture of this length.

He himself occasionally indicates the need to show consideration. He defends those people in his entourage who negotiate on his behalf, in other words, those who have to cancel his engagements or decline invitations. He defends those who make themselves unpopular on his behalf. 'Everyone is annoyed with Märkle. I know they are, and he knows, too. But that's how it has to be. If people are not annoyed with him, it means things are not going well for me.' Dr Uli Märkle is the person responsible for making Karajan's music films, in other words, he is a central figure in what is still called Karajan's empire. Is he also still Karajan's spokesman? Neither he nor the conductor will express an opinion on this question, there is a sense of loyalty between them, and this has to satisfy everyone's curiosity.

Old age and the various complaints that have often been mentioned have made Herbert von Karajan considerably less mobile but certainly not incapable of movement. Time and again one is struck at concerts by the way in which he can still bring up his arms to underline a point of musical emphasis. And, in much the same way, one is astonished in conversation

28

with him by a degree of commitment expressed that one neither expected nor hoped for. He can still get annoyed, he can still give instructions by telephone with glacial politeness, he still has no difficulty working out what is going on in the world of music, and he reacts swiftly and effectively, often to the amazement of younger or apparently more nimble conductors.

He has allowed a few layers of his personality to be peeled away. He now admits that he keeps himself informed about current affairs by watching television and reading newspapers. He is prepared to talk about reviews as though he had actually read them. He no longer considers it necessary to act as though his head were in the clouds. By his own lights, he has grown more realistic, and therefore more human. By his own lights, of course, he is, and remains, Herbert von Karajan, and leaves people in no doubt that he cannot tolerate criticism. The most he is prepared to admit is that, 'I sometimes listen to my colleagues' opinions. But they have to do what I consider to be correct. I do not like to be contradicted.'

This needs to be placed in context. In practical matters such as a production or a rehearsal, he is prepared to come to a prompt understanding even with a simple stagehand and to agree, if need be, with the latter's objections. He respects those who have practical experience in whatever area, as long as he has recognized their particular competence. But he does not appreciate discussions in an area where he himself is the acknowledged authority. There may be other views, but the only one that matters to him is his own.

'The season in Ulm always ended in April. I returned home, studied my repertoire, and began to get involved in the Festival and to watch the great conductors – and I went to Bayreuth to see the great Wagner performances under Toscanini.'

What Karajan most remembers from his whole time in Ulm is the fact that he spent the long summer holidays in Salzburg and Bayreuth, surviving on the most modest means and recovering from the almost physical exertions of his artistic activity in Ulm. His intimate knowledge of the Salzburg Festival dates from these years, as, by his own admission, do his meetings with Max Reinhardt and Egon Friedell, and, of course, he has no difficulty in explaining that his constant attendance at all the rehearsals and performances in Salzburg allowed him to go through his own repertory with the same degree of inspiration that he brought to his tentative experiments in the theatre in Ulm.

There is one incident which must have taken place towards the end of Karajan's time in Ulm and which he knows he has already recounted on many occasions. But it is important to him because it underlines a particular point: 'I have often told the story of how I returned to Ulm after a summer in Bayreuth and how the orchestral players simply played better than they had done before. Because they sensed that I now had higher expectations.'

If Karajan tells this story at all, and tells it, moreover, at various times virtually unchanged, it finally becomes clear what he means. For him it confirms the conductor's influence on an orchestra, an influence that must be located beyond his precise ideas on music and beyond his professional expertise. He argues – and every orchestral musician in the world would agree with him – that, in addition to his other, difficult basic duties, a conductor also has the task of inspiring an orchestra. He argues that he must be able to convey a sense of 'magic', a word which Karajan himself uses in precisely this context.

'I simply made different, greater demands after I had heard Toscanini in Bayreuth. And the orchestra attempted to fulfil those demands.' The committed music lover, ever reluctant to get involved in such discussions, will no doubt accept Karajan's claim uncritically. The long-standing professional observer of concert rehearsals and performances throughout the world can only confirm Karajan's apparently odd remark. For while it is true that musicians expect their conductor to give them the simple technical help which the man with the baton can offer, they also expect him to give them something extra when it comes to the concert itself. They themselves call it inspiration and freely admit that they play better under an inspired conductor. In other words, they confirm what Karajan says. They know from experience that they need a conductor who, no matter how difficult he may be, brings to the podium the highest demands and a rare sense of vision.

30

During his so-called heyday, Karajan conducted orchestras throughout the world, and he knows exactly how to handle musicians. Now that he concentrates basically on the Berlin and Vienna Philharmonics, he also knows that, however familiar he is with these ensembles, his rehearsals must not be routine but that he must always bring a sense of inspiration to them. This, too, is something about which he speaks at length, with his unique mixture of specialist knowledge and the philosophy he has developed as a conductor. Though not when he talks about Ulm. Of course, he still remembers his one good colleague there and the intendant who engaged him on the spot in Salzburg, but he cannot talk in a relaxed way about his memories of the singers and musicians in Ulm. Even in 1930 he did not want to hear them in reality. In 1987 he still cannot talk about them without regret. And his profound awareness that it was in towns like Ulm that he and many conductors of his generation learned their trade in the only acceptable way vanishes into thin air when he thinks that similar conditions still exist today.

'The whole world has changed, nowadays records and television have raised the expectations of music lovers everywhere, even in the smallest towns and villages, so that they are no longer satisfied with a theatre like the one in Ulm. At least, they don't have to be satisfied with it.'

For Herbert von Karajan the end in Ulm came almost as a surprise. 'At the end of my eighth season in Ulm there was still the same intendant who had signed me up in Salzburg. He simply dismissed me. He said, "I don't want you back here at the end of this summer. Next season we'll probably be giving the same operas that you have already conducted here. You've learned all you could learn in Ulm. It's time for you to move on. You'll either go to the dogs or else you'll make a career for yourself – as I firmly believe. But you can't come back here."' Harsh words must certainly have been spoken, for Karajan often recalls the conversation, and whenever he recounts it, he always mentions the other alternative of 'going to the dogs'. 'I was thrown out, there's no other way of looking at it. I'd not been offered another position. And there were no vacant jobs anywhere in Germany. But I sensed that he was serious and that he believed I would make a career for myself. And later, when I had been taken on in Aachen and was already conducting in Berlin, I received a letter of congratulations from Ulm. But I had a difficult summer ahead of me before I reached that stage.'

Aachen and Berlin

'I normally returned home in May. But this time there was no point. So I went to Berlin to look for a job. I went to all the agencies and accompanied singers at the biggest of them all, the Paritätischer Bühnennachweis. I hoped all the time that an intendant would not only find the singers he wanted for the coming season, but that he would also notice me. But for three months absolutely nothing happened. There was not a thing happening as far as I was concerned. No one needed a conductor. No one discussed business with me. Every post in Germany seemed to have been filled. I was the only conductor in Berlin who did not have a contract for the coming season, or so, at least, it appeared.'

And so, before Karajan could become what he wanted to be, and before he could do what he dreamed of doing, he had to spend a whole summer in Berlin, a time which he himself describes as depressing when, by his own account, he was the only unemployed conductor in Berlin waiting to be taken on. It was also a test of his willpower, something he rarely talks about but which he relies on in exceptional circumstances: 'Finally the Aachen intendant came to Berlin. I discovered this from my agent. I asked to speak to him. I hypnotized him, saying, "I won't let you go until you take me on". I had told myself that I must get something out of this interview. And my opposite number must have sensed how much I was under this constraint. Of course, the season in Aachen, too, was already over, so he could not ask me to conduct a trial performance. But he invited me to an orchestra rehearsal.'

In Aachen there was a repetition – if Karajan's account may be believed – of what had happened at his first rehearsal in the

33

presence of his professors at the Vienna Academy, and of what was to happen with all the great orchestras which he wanted to get to know through making an initial striking impression. 'And so I had only one rehearsal in Aachen, with no concert to follow. The musical life of the town was organized in such a way that there was an independent conductor who conducted the Aachen Orchestra and who took the musicians for a certain number of concerts and rehearsals. On the other evenings, the orchestra performed in the opera house, when the general music director, who was himself answerable to the Aachen intendant, took charge. For the orchestra, however, there was also a kind of general secretary, a former member of the Berlin Philharmonic, who had taken early retirement in Berlin in order to take up his appointment here. And he was present, of course, at the rehearsal which I had to conduct. I still remember quite clearly how the musicians came up to him afterwards and told him they had imagined a different kind of conductor. But he had realized how I worked, and he explained to them that I was the right man for them. And so I was taken on.'

If Karajan recalls the first rehearsals which he holds on these occasions, it is always with reference to the few bars that he goes through with an orchestra in order to show the old hands among them that their playing has long since become smudged and imprecise, and that the conductor's task at a rehearsal is to insist that the notes be played 'at their full length' and, needless to say, with precision. Karajan always gives the impression that what is involved here is an entirely technical appeal to the authentic note values. That it is, of course, first and foremost a question of demanding one hundred per cent commitment from his musicians is something he does not elaborate in detail. It looks as though passages on how one approaches music as a conductor and how one communicates such ideas to an orchestra are intended for the by now legendary book he keeps on promising to write on the subject. It looks as though he will write about this in great detail, or else that he will take his 'secrets' (which do not appear so mysterious to him) to the grave.

But before Aachen could appoint him their general music director (a position which, in the eyes of the world, he was to hold for some time afterwards), and before he could begin to look round for more important positions in Berlin and elsewhere, he had to conduct a trial rehearsal which found little favour with the Aachen orchestral musicians, even if it impressed a shrewd orchestral player from Berlin. He also had to build up his position in the concert hall and in the theatre with sufficient care to make the then general music director Peter Raabe realize that he was being ousted by a younger colleague. Raabe, who was later elected president of the Reichsmusikkammer in Berlin, left no perceptible trace on Karajan's memory and was clearly not of sufficient interest as a musician to be a rival, then or in the future.

Karajan himself depicts the situation today in extremely simple terms. 'I wanted to avoid all conflict with my rival. After I had been in Aachen for six months, the post of general music director fell vacant in Karlsruhe, and so I conducted there, was successful, and was offered the job. That was the moment when everything was decided for me in Aachen. The mayor offered me the job for the coming season, Raabe felt betrayed and went to Berlin. And I became boss.'

The word 'boss' recurs time and again in connection with Karajan. In virtually all the opera houses and institutions where he has worked he has only ever been described as 'boss', as he knows for himself and as he has accepted. For him the description means work and responsibility, certainly not an honour or a distinction, but something of a burden instead. Whatever else one wishes to include under this term, Karajan is happy that it should be so, accepting that in his capacity as boss he may be reproached for decisions which are not in fact his. That, too, is part of the job. According to Karajan's understanding of the term, a boss assumes total and complete responsibility for everything.

The morning on which Herbert von Karajan described the situation in Aachen to me was pleasant and sunny, interrupted by odd telephone calls with Berlin: the Philharmonic's artistic director spoke in his inimitably authoritative way with the manager of his orchestra. He asked about this or that instrumentalist, and when he mentioned that at the next concert he would like such and such a player at the first desk, it sounded like a polite suggestion, but was clearly meant as an order which admitted of no dissent. As indeed it was, for the days when large autonomous orchestras could afford to ignore a polite request on the part of Herbert von Karajan are long since past. Here was Karajan on the telephone, working out in his head the particular sound he wanted to hear from his orchestra in Berlin when they played the concert in question, perhaps some months away in the future, and all these suggestions were being noted down and acted on in Berlin. Karajan accepted it all as a matter of course, and then went on to tell of the weeks and months when, for the one and only time in his life, he had felt like giving up all hope. Months during which he accompanied sopranos and tenors as they auditioned for opera house intendants, and he himself did not get a look-in. He simply did not have a contract for the coming season . . .

After Ulm and the deprivations of a summer spent in Berlin, it will come as no surprise (but surprises are scarcely to be expected in a biography about Herbert von Karajan) to learn that he was offered, and accepted, a special post in Aachen.

At this point I must intervene in the narrative and point out that Karajan spoke spontaneously and without any prompting not only about the difficulties he had in obtaining this position but also about the well-known political implications.

This, I had thought previously, was a particularly difficult obstacle which could lead to the breakdown of all relations between us: all too often and all too insistently earlier writers have enquired into Herbert von Karajan's political past at the time of the National Socialist movement. All the relevant books have quoted the membership numbers which he was given on being accepted into the party, first in Salzburg and then in Aachen. And all his public engagements which, because of the programme or audience, could be described as labours of love performed for the sake of the party have been listed in special studies. Earlier biographers either passed lightly over the subject, or else they sank their teeth, with grim determination, into this bone of contention, refusing to let it go until they had established the full extent of Karajan's links with the

36

NSDAP* during these years, including his links with Nazi ideas and with their protagonists. By the time that I found myself sitting in Salzburg one cool morning in 1987, with the subject of Herbert von Karajan in Aachen at the head of the agenda, there was not a crime of which the conductor did not stand indicted.

And Karajan?

He broached the subject himself, and everyone will understand if what he wanted to say is reproduced unabridged and word for word.

'Of course, the time of which we are now speaking was a very political time. I also understand why people continue to write about it and puzzle over it. But I want to say something myself about this one particular detail in my career. For I think it is important for people to read my own point of view for once. I was about to be appointed general music director in Aachen when the district governor came to me and said, "Well, you are to be made general music director. But you'll also have to be a party member . . .". And that is basically the entire story of my party membership, whatever people have tried to make of it subsequently. Even today there's nothing else I can say on the subject, though I may still be misunderstood if I attempt to explain it. But after the months of despair when I was waiting for a contract in Berlin, after all the efforts of obtaining one in Aachen, and in view of the position I was hoping for, I would probably have met completely different conditions in order to get it. It is sometimes said, unthinkingly, that I would have sold my own grandmother to get this position. Yet this sentence sums up fairly accurately what I was capable of doing at that time, young, hungry conductor that I was.

'Entry into the party was a condition of my becoming general music director in Aachen. For me it was the price you sometimes have to pay to get exactly what you want if there is a particular goal you must achieve at all costs. Let me give you an example: many, many years later in Switzerland, when I wanted to take a particular route over a certain mountain and to have my own

* National Socialist Workers' Party

37

guide, I was told it was possible but that I would also have to pay an additional fee to another, local guide. I gave him the money and did what I wanted.

'Of course, a generation has now grown up which can no longer imagine such things and which likes to pass judgement, particularly on a period which they themselves never knew. We know all the debates, we've heard and seen them countless times – I think they are all false and misleading, since I can see they don't lead us anywhere any longer. The present generation may be deeply interested in our past. But they can have no idea of what it felt like to be a musician at that time, seeing a goal and having the means to achieve that goal. I refused to get involved in debates on the subject after the war, and kept silent, and basically I still refuse to get involved in debates today. I can see no point, for example, in giving a detailed description of the difficult situation to which I was exposed under the Third Reich. I never refer to how difficult it has been in Germany recently for me and my wife. That, too, is something the younger generation knows practically nothing about, they can have no idea of what it has been like. This question has been asked of me countless times, but for me it was answered long ago and does not need a new answer: I became boss in Aachen and could conduct according to my own ideas.'

This, then, is Herbert von Karajan's reply, as explicit as it is personal. He himself is anything but unworldly and is certainly not of the view that his attitude will not be noted with particular attention today. Yet he has never once referred to the fact that the 1987/8 theatre season in Vienna began with a production staged by George Tabori's 'Der Kreis' theatre company. The play was called *Born Guilty* and dealt exclusively with young people who want to sort out in their own minds whether their fathers or grandfathers became involved in the machinery of National Socialism and, if so, to what extent they were active elements in that machinery. Herbert von Karajan's daughter made her stage debut in this production as a member of the Tabori company and was acclaimed as a highly talented actress.

'Under the system that was then in force the position of general music director was a good deal more important than can perhaps

38

be imagined today. Above all, it meant a great deal of work and responsibility. Our orchestra was made up of approximately seventy players, but could always be increased to the size of a normal symphony orchestra. Each season I had to rehearse and conduct six subscription concerts and eight popular concerts. In the opera house I superintended between four and six new productions each season and conducted all the performances myself. I was responsible for both the concert programming and also for the choice of operas. In the theatre the intendant was of course responsible for the budget. But apart from that, he never interfered with my plans. Guest conductors of the kind that are now normal in any cycle of concerts were virtually non-existent with us. I recall once having invited Willem Mengelberg because he was being talked about all over Germany. We became friendly during his visit to Aachen and always got along with each other afterwards – but these concerts were exceptions and had no special repercussions. The orchestra was used to being under one person, and the system of general music director was planned entirely with this in mind. He was a man who had been elected and who in turn was responsible for the musical life of the town.'

Aachen not only had a great tradition as a centre of music, it also had a correspondingly well-informed public and enough wealthy industrialists to act as patrons. And it was a town from where conductors could be invited to take up interesting challenges elsewhere. By contemporary standards Herbert von Karajan had risen with uncommon speed to a position commensurate with his abilities.

'It was in Aachen that I first began to produce. I'd been there for four years when I produced my first opera, *The Mastersingers of Nuremberg*. For me this was not a question of launching out in some new direction, it was an entirely natural reaction on the part of a musician to a situation which arises time and again in every opera house in the world, when a conductor notices during the rehearsals that the producer he's working with does not know the work he's producing. And of course a conductor always notices when a producer with whom he is yoked together understands far too little about the music and about the singers with whom he has to work. That sort of situation arises at every rehearsal. A producer simply cannot understand why a chorus can't sing *pianissimo* at the same time as performing complicated movements on stage. A producer never has adequate understanding of the fact that there are moments in a singer's life on stage when he has to concentrate on the music and not on the producer's eccentric stage directions. Sometimes one attempts, as conductor, to explain this to the producer and to reach a compromise. In my own case the situation never led to any compromises. I simply had to become a producer myself in order to solve the problems involved.

'Of course, this was by no means usual at that time. It is said of Toscanini that he, too, acted as producer. But that's not entirely accurate. I know, because I saw him at countless rehearsals in Salzburg. He had his own ideas about what should happen on stage; he was the maestro and everyone else had to fit in with him. But there was always a producer there who did the actual work, and even if, as I still remember, Toscanini was dissatisfied with his apparently preferred Salzburg producer, there was still a producer, and Toscanini did not draw the same logical conclusion that I did from his feeling of dissatisfaction. In any case, it was never entirely clear what exactly *would* have satisfied him. But there was one occasion when he was in complete agreement with a producer – it was the time he conducted *Tannhäuser* in Bayreuth and the producer was Siegfried Wagner. I attended the rehearsals and the performances, and what I remember is not a production that was in any way exceptional, but a musical interpretation which was so well balanced and so fascinating that you really could not imagine a better production. It was the satisfied conductor who in the final analysis was responsible for a perfect performance. The producer did not get in the way, it was perfect as it was.'

The subject of opera production is one that enjoys a special significance for Herbert von Karajan, as the artist himself knows and explains. He has his own views and, of course, his own opinions on what is currently described as modern opera theatre and on the popularity of music theatre. We shall return to this point. For the time being, however, we are still in Aachen, where a young general music director, deeply influenced by

40

Max Reinhardt, breaks with tradition and turns, successfully, to producing operas.

Karajan looks back on this period with visible pleasure and, as before, is consistent in excluding the so-called private factor from his account. He gives the impression that in Aachen, as elsewhere, his life was devoted solely to work – which is no doubt not far from the truth. And he is consistent in his way of attaching importance, retrospectively, to what remains in his memory of that period, such as the fact that he himself turned to producing, that he himself chose his operas and concert programmes, that he accepted only those invitations which promised more than simply an out-of-town concert, and that he was in charge for the first time, and happily so.

'Our concert programmes in Aachen were certainly not what you'd call conservative today. But they were put together for an audience which, as a general rule, *was* conservative, which was unenthusiastic about contemporary music and which reacted in more or less the way that we've all been used to seeing until very recently. In other words, even at that time the subscription audience arrived late on purpose, preferring to miss the first piece, since they knew it was new music. Of course, it was music by what was then the younger generation of German composers, music by Orff, Egk and Fortner above all. Of course, I rehearsed this music with the same degree of seriousness as every other piece on the programme, and of course I never won friends by doing so. Not in Aachen and not in Vienna either – I still remember conducting a subscription concert for the Philharmonic around 1960 which included a piece by Anton von Webern: the subscribers talked and coughed and laughed throughout the piece, and certainly did not think that this sort of music should be performed in the Musikvereinssaal.

'But I have always preferred to take up works into my repertory only when I felt I was ready for them. I'm thinking, for example, of how long it took before I found the right relationship to Gustav Mahler, and the wonderful reception our performances with the Berlin Philharmonic were then given. And I can still recall as though it were yesterday my work with the orchestra when we finally recorded an album of works by the Second

41

Viennese School. I kept on telling the players that it was utterly wrong to perform this type of music "differently" from any so-called traditional piece. We spent an eternity polishing up these recordings, it was my ambition to make Schoenberg sound exactly like Mozart or Beethoven. And believe it or not, this set of records was not only an artistic success, it was a financial one, too. Of course, I'm not claiming that we'd turned Schoenberg, Berg and Webern into popular composers with a new and wider public, but I believe our approach to this kind of music was understood and respected. Whatever people may write about me, I have never shut myself off from contemporary music.

'I have never made any secret of my attitude towards new music, and I have always been successful whenever I have thrown my weight behind a new piece.'

Herbert von Karajan is no archivist. Whenever he attempts to look into the past, it is without the aid of a notebook or even a collection of programmes. He is happy to leave other people to do the research, and shows genuine delight when reminded of something he himself had apparently long since forgotten. He performed contemporary music not only in Aachen and later in Berlin, but even during his legendary period of management at the Vienna State Opera where local and world premières were prepared with all the expense of great first nights. Of course, neither Frank Martin nor Benjamin Britten was regarded as a great innovator at that time, but they were certainly contemporary composers, and *Der Sturm* and *A Midsummer Night's Dream* were performances that were mounted with all the commitment of a major institution and which did find an audience for themselves.

And as for the traditional inclusion of recent works in the Salzburg Festival programme, Herbert von Karajan has not of course relied entirely on his own initiative to commission new works during the course of the last few decades, but he has recently familiarized himself with award procedures and has also undertaken on-the-spot investigations into the actual preparations involved. He has his own very personal views on this subject, views which are certainly not directed against modern composers, but which are concerned exclusively with

42

an optimal presentation that, to Karajan's way of thinking, has not always been adequately discussed in the past.

There is no point in trying to present Herbert von Karajan now as a great innovator in music. That, in any case, is not what he has in mind. But it would be equally wrong to denounce the conductor as quintessentially conservative. Certainly, he does not see himself in such terms and argues that in his day he has had contact, where appropriate, with contemporary composers. And this is something no one will deny.

Another brief word about politics.

'National Socialism had no particular influence on the concert programmes that we gave in Aachen. Of course, there were the general restrictions, and of course, the responsible bodies in the capital Berlin were somewhat more liberal-minded than the local authorities in Aachen. But both in Aachen and Berlin it was possible to oppose restrictions that had once been imposed. I know it's perhaps not the best example, but I remember the district governor once wanted to prevent us from performing the St Matthew Passion in Aachen. On that occasion I was quick to react and asked to see the Reichsmusikkammer document which stated that passiontide music could not be performed. There was no such document and we were able to go ahead with the performance unhindered.

'I am not claiming that politics had not penetrated the world of music. That would be wrong, and there are plenty of documents to refute such a claim. But it would also be wrong to think that we musicians thought only in political categories at that time. Then, as now, we were musicians and artists, and we discussed musical, artistic questions. And, of course, even at that time, musical intrigue was not necessarily thought of as a political act, it was generally the sort of intrigue you find among musicians and artists in every age and under every form of government.'

When, in spite of everything, Herbert von Karajan talks about the National Socialist past, it is with the palpable aim of bringing home to young people the fact that he at least considers it inadmissible to ignore all other aspects and to consider only the restrictions, the services rendered to the party, and the political engagements. He wants people to remember that even at that time he was involved in making music and he asks, with some plausibility, that they consider the fact that preparations had to be made for opera productions and concerts. At the time when these conversations were being recorded, Karajan was aware, as an observer, of the whole discussion that was taking place on television about the past and the Austrian President's attempts to come to terms with his role in it. His comments were brief. He considered the discussion to be basically unproductive.

'It was 1937 when the first enquiry came from Vienna. I'm sure the reason for the invitation was because I was friendly with the director Erwin Fischer from my Salzburg days and because Bruno Walter wanted to meet me. I was offered *Tristan and Isolde* and promised two, no, three orchestra rehearsals. I was delighted to accept. Two weeks before the performance I received a letter from Vienna, saying that there were many changes being made in the theatre and that I could have only two rehearsals. A week before the performance another letter arrived from Vienna, explaining that there were difficulties with the preparations for a Philharmonic concert and that there was now going to be only one orchestral rehearsal. And then when I arrived in Vienna, the leader of the orchestra tried to do what orchestra players have always tried to do with young conductors. He told me, "You'll not achieve anything with a single orchestra rehearsal. Do without the rehearsal. If you come to the performance well prepared, it's enough to know that we, too, are well prepared. And believe me, we'll play as well for you as we do for our best conductors." And so I swallowed this suggestion, too, and made do with a piano rehearsal with the singers. But even that was indescribable and I still remember it vividly. The woman who was singing Brangäne did not come at all, but sent an apology. The woman singing Isolde used the rehearsal to deal with her correspondence and only marked a few entries in passing . . . And yet the performance itself was very good and a great personal success for me, but I told myself at the time that I would not conduct again in Vienna until the time was ripe for me. And for many, many years I did not conduct at the State Opera again. I was wiser for the experience.'

Neither in the tone of his voice nor in the accompanying

gestures does Karajan relate this story about his first encounter as a conductor with the Vienna Opera reproachfully or resentfully. That's how it was at the time. He insists that that is how young conductors were always treated in the larger theatres, and he himself was merely a young conductor at that time. He could have reacted differently and played along, so that he would soon have been invited back. The fact that he did not do so and that he adopted a different approach in future when conducting negotiations with those major opera houses that commanded respect was a matter of course for him. Above all because such negotiations always ended successfully for him. He has often told the corresponding story of his invitation to Berlin, including his first appearance there and the decisive review that followed, describing him as 'The Karajan miracle'. It is a classic example of the way in which one must be convinced of one's own merits and aware of what one's first appearance might entail when conducting negotiations.

'It was the following year, 1938, that my enervating correspondence with Berlin began. I received a letter written on behalf of the general intendant Heinz Tietjen, asking whether I would be interested in conducting the première of an opera by Wagner-Régeny at the State Opera. The work in question was *Die Bürger von Calais*. It was the sort of letter that you could see had been written from on high. It came almost straight from Olympus and was written in a tone which I did not like – I still do not like this condescending tone. My reaction was to reply not directly but, like the other letter, through a third party. My agent wrote, very politely of course, to say that the offer was an honour for me, but that, before conducting a world première in Berlin, I should like to introduce myself to local audiences by means of three operas, *Fidelio*, *Tristan and Isolde* and *The Mastersingers of Nuremberg*.

'Another letter arrived from Tietjen's subordinate saying that there could be no question of an advance engagement, and that these three operas in particular were works which the general intendant had personally staged and conducted. I then had a letter sent in return, thanking Herr Tietjen profusely, but saying that in the circumstances I should prefer not to conduct the world première in Berlin.

'The correspondence between Berlin and Aachen continued, never less than polite and diplomatic, but always signed by subordinates. "Herr Tietjen offers you a revival of *Carmen* with a first-class cast." "Herr von Karajan feels honoured. He asks to be informed what Herr Tietjen means by a first-class cast." Back came the reply that this varied from case to case, and so I wrote to inform him that in my own case it was better if I waited before making my debut with the State Opera. It was at that point that I received the first personal letter from the great Tietjen himself. He wrote that he was curious to find someone so determined to have his own way. "I am writing to offer you the opera *Tannhäuser*, as you requested." Now I, too, could finally reply in person. "Thank you for the confidence you have placed in me. However, it was not *Tannhäuser* that I demanded but *Fidelio*, *Tristan* and *The Mastersingers*." Tietjen's reaction to this letter was, "You shall have your way".'

For this book alone Herbert von Karajan has recorded this story at least twice. On each occasion the content was identical, even the intonation was the same as he read out letters as though they still existed. Never for a moment was there any suggestion that he looked back on this battle of strength as a source of amusement. He told the story as though it were a parable, a didactic tale he wanted properly understood. The post of general music director in Aachen was a thoroughly respectable one. An engagement in Berlin with three major operas was his chance of achieving a rapid breakthrough and reaching the absolute summit. It was this or nothing as far as Karajan was concerned. He wanted to be able to count on the audience's undivided attention and not have to develop slowly from one guest engagement to another, with the performance of what was then a contemporary opera. 'If you set out looking for compromise, you've already lost', is his comment forty years after this particular victory. Not even at the first rehearsals for *Fidelio* did he agree to any compromise, but adopted a tone of extreme politeness towards an orchestra which played 'as though they were all wearing starched collars'. It was at these rehearsals that the battle was decided in his favour, he convinced the players and won Tietjen's respect. The latter wanted to know, of course, what sort of a person he had taken on. *Fidelio* was followed in fact by *Tristan and Isolde*, and after the performance on 21 October 1938 the *B.Z. am Mittag* published a review under the title, 'At the State Opera: the Karajan miracle'.

Times have changed since then, the title of the review is now the title of a book about Herbert von Karajan, and it has been used throughout the world as a quotation. And on each occasion it was recalled that the admiration felt for Karajan also included a note of clear aggression towards Wilhelm Furtwängler.

It is finally impossible to defer mentioning a name which is so much a part of Karajan's history. Anyone who has had the opportunity over the decades to listen to Karajan's comments on Furtwängler must be honest with himself and admit that his attitude has not always been what it is now. It has taken many, many years to reach the point that Karajan has now reached, where he can comment as follows on a quite unique relationship:

'Of course, it was clear from the outset, even to me, that Tietjen and the critic van der Nüll were playing me off against Wilhelm Furtwängler. I was even told as much in the opera house. Tietjen, who was himself an exceptional person and who thought he was a law unto himself, had difficulty dealing with Furtwängler and told me he was no longer prepared to put up with these difficulties. He said, "On the day when Furtwängler comes back to the State Opera, I shall leave the building through the back door." Of course, he did not keep his word, he could ill afford to have done so. But his animosity was great and always in evidence. And almost all the stories that are still told about Berlin in 1938 are completely true. Furtwängler had a hard struggle on his hands, and I was used to make life difficult for him. There were vicious intrigues against him, and I was useful to his opponents as the young, unspoilt rival. That can't be denied. And I think it's entirely understandable that Furtwängler suffered from it much more than I did. Until then he had been in undisputed control. And then I came along, the young man who had nothing to lose. My age alone must have been enough to annoy him.

'However, it is wrong to see the conflicts between us from a political point of view. The difficulties which Furtwängler had with the Party had nothing to do with me. What took place between us could have taken place at any time and in any country. It was the sort of rivalry that is bound to exist between two conductors, when one of them is at the height of his career and the other comes along with all the innocence of youth. For my own part I was really not interested in playing along with some vicious intrigue. I wanted to seize all the opportunities offered me to be able to conduct. And every opportunity that presented itself in Berlin meant that Furtwängler suffered as a result.

'To begin with, that was the least of my worries. For immediately after I'd conducted *Tristan*, Tietjen introduced me to Gustaf Gründgens. He had spent four years looking for a conductor with whom to do *The Magic Flute*. And he offered me this chance. It was a wonderful offer, but I could see no way of reconciling it with my commitments in Aachen. And Tietjen, who declared that the whole affair could be resolved by a single telephone call from the Ministry, simply did not understand the situation I was in. The problem for me was not the dates of rehearsals or performances, but that I needed two months to think over such an important project. When Gründgens discovered my reasons, he found my attitude very much to his liking. We found the necessary time and then began the rehearsals, which were a time of sheer delight for me.'

When Karajan talks about rehearsing with Gründgens, his eyes light up and he insists on relating hundreds of details in order to make his enthusiasm more explicable. For him it is still important to remind his public that he is not simply the conductor who refuses to work with producers. After all, Karajan attended Max Reinhardt's legendary rehearsals in Salzburg. He worked in excellent harmony with Gustaf Gründgens – and years later invited the producer to Salzburg. One of his most famous opera productions was with Franco Zeffirelli, a joint production of *La Bohème* which he conducted in more than one opera house. He saw and experienced difficulties only with producers whom he reckoned to be second-rate. And he intentionally avoids producers who, in his view, wish to serve something other than the music. He is familiar with them and knows what he is talking about when he says he does not always stay to the end of their productions. He does not work with them, he does not recommend them when they are being discussed. He prefers instead to enthuse about Reinhardt and Gründgens, and he knows very well that this, too, is a way of criticizing other producers.

'I was right to prepare for this production with Gründgens. It was pure joy working with him. He was a master of his art and knew exactly what he wanted to show with his production. It was not the Prince, but Papageno who became the central character in the opera, a figure whom Gründgens himself expressly described at the time as the typical Austrian. He glorified Papageno – which, of course, was also a political statement in its way – Papageno, the character who wanted nothing more than enough to eat and a girl of his own. The key sentence in his production seemed to him to be Papageno's line, "Fighting's not my business".'

Unlike other artists who are nowadays to be heard describing the inner resistance they felt towards National Socialism, Karajan talks instead about his former colleagues, describing the way they behaved at rehearsals: 'Gründgens was always making violent and obscene remarks about the Third Reich, although he was regarded as a favourite of the National Socialists, he could never stop himself from making the most public remarks. I still remember very clearly rehearsing one of the scenes in which Sarastro turns to the priests: "We don't need that kind of unctuous tone here. Keep it for one of the Party's instruction courses."'

And again, 'What I learned most of all from Gründgens is that you can achieve thrilling theatrical effects very quietly, without any grand gestures. An example? In *Tosca*, for instance, the Scarpia doesn't need to play the villain all the time. He doesn't have to show us how everyone trembles in his presence, it's enough for him to be there and for him to be surrounded by fear. And finally, in his big scene with Tosca, he doesn't have to strike the table in her presence and raise his voice, he should speak very quietly when giving the final order for Caravadossi to be tortured. He must sing his "Tutto" so quietly that you think he's lost his voice, only then do the opera and the character work. And everyone in the audience senses what Puccini meant. What I learned as a producer from Gründgens can be used in any opera, you can always manage with what appear to be very low-key effects, but you'll achieve more impact than through any amount of grand gestures and running around. But it goes without saying that, after you've worked as a conductor with a man like Gründgens, you'll not enjoy working with second-class producers. And so it is people like Gustaf Gründgens whom I am bound to hold responsible for the fact that, since then, I have always directed my own productions.'

Half a century has gone by since this *Magic Flute* was performed under Karajan, Gründgens and the designer Traugott Müller, and yet not only in Berlin but elsewhere, too, older opera lovers and *cognoscenti* continue to speak enthusiastically about it. And the fact that Karajan has not been consistent in his attitude, but has staged *The Magic Flute* on many subsequent occasions with other producers does not detract from what he has to say or rob his words of the weight that is due to them. His most recent attempt to stage the work was at the Salzburg Festival with Giorgio Strehler and Luciano Damiani. The attempt was a failure for several reasons, but at least it was confirmation of the quality requirement of which Karajan speaks. When he invited them to work with him, Strehler and Damiani enjoyed just as high a reputation as their great predecessors.

Among Karajan's outstanding characteristics, however, is his refusal to seek public scapegoats for the failures in his life. This may be ascribed either to self-regard or else to a certain disregard for the general public as represented by critics and reporters – although far worse interpretations than these have been offered for his attitude. But having observed Karajan at close hand over a period, I would claim that he is simply not interested in conducting post mortems on less than wholly successful productions or in discussing who, for whatever reasons, may not have achieved what was expected of them. Karajan will long since have been working on his next production and has thoughts only for that. Only much later, years later, does he think again about a performance or a film which was not to his taste. By then he will have a film of it in his private archives

50

and can run through it on his own. It will serve as an example of something which failed and which is not allowed to fail in the same way again.

Karajan's great success in Berlin, the immediate confirmation of his special status in the capital of the Third Reich, and Tietjen's offers to allow him to concentrate on further operatic productions were clearly not sufficiently secure for him to give up a position in which he was still the undisputed boss. 'I did not simply leave Aachen. I wanted to stay the full length of my contract, conducting and producing. An agreement with Tietjen seemed entirely possible at that time. I was appointed State Conductor and was given a contract for twenty-five performances; they were very generous and would have offered me more. And this, remember, at a time when any conductor could have been summoned to Berlin from the provinces without difficulty, when the Ministry was prepared to annul every valid contract in favour of work in Berlin. I'm certain anyone else would simply have remained in Berlin. But I also wanted to remain in Aachen, and even this was granted to me. There then began a period for me when I was permanently on the road. A period in which I learned to plan my time with great precision. I spent three days in Berlin, then took the night train to Aachen and went straight from the station to the first rehearsal. I then spent ten days in Aachen, rehearsing and performing, at the end of which I was again back on the train to Berlin. There was a real sense of rhythm, it was tiring of course, but it gave me the feeling that I was needed in both places. The strain could be borne, and I was happy to accept it. For me, it was very important not to sell myself straightaway to Tietjen and to Berlin. I was left with enough self-respect.'

How serious Karajan felt about his self-respect at that time is clear from his words, still tinged with a sense of slight bitterness, 'In spite of that, my work in Aachen came to an end, and it did so, moreover, against my will, behind my back. The Aachen intendant signed up a new conductor, something I discovered when I was in Berlin. I was enormously offended; most of all, of course, because he'd not talked to me about it first. Otto Kirchner, the intendant, explained to me why he did it, but not until much later, after the war. I'm supposed to understand now, but I have never really been able to understand why he did it.'

From the viewpoint of the people of Aachen Herbert von Karajan was already a Berliner who was bound to reduce his commitments in the town and carry them out halfheartedly. And one day, of course, he would move to Berlin for good. And so they took precautionary measures and made the 'break' which Karajan himself did not yet dare make. In Aachen they wanted a musician fully committed to the town, and so they sent Karajan packing before his contract had expired. Karajan himself raises a quiet word of dissent: 'That's not how I remember the situation. I knew what a dangerous place Berlin was, I continued to take my work in Aachen seriously. Even today I cannot accept that the intendant, Kirchner, was right. Even so, when we talked things over later, I was able to tell him that I understood his motives. Our relations were back to normal. But that was the most one could say.' And, as he reminisces about his departure from Aachen and the beginning of his time in Berlin, Karajan is proved right, in his way, with his interpretation of events, since he was exposed from the very outset to the permanent rivalry of Furtwängler and, as he had expected, he did not really get on with Tietjen.

'The tensions in my relationship with Tietjen began very early but they're easily explained. He could not keep his word and had to allow Furtwängler back on the podium. He could not be happy with a conductor who also wanted to produce and so trespass on the general intendant's preserves. And, of course, he didn't like me for wanting to influence the casting: here, too, I crossed his path, *his* path most of all. Until then Tietjen had been the undisputed *éminence grise* of the world of music – as far as the general public were concerned he was generally so invisible that people often asked jokingly whether Tietjen actually existed. At the same time, however, he was masterful in his dealings with power, with ministries and with important people in the Party, he wasn't used to other people having their own opinions on anything and wanting to assert themselves.

'I know of two instances of the way in which Tietjen really harmed me. When Karl Böhm moved from Dresden to Vienna,

I wanted to apply for his post. I went to Tietjen and told him so. I'd have been prepared to continue conducting in Berlin, but I wanted to find out what I, on my own, could get out of a large high-ranking opera house with the capacity of the Dresden Opera. I believed at the time that I was the right age and that I had the necessary maturity for the position. Tietjen listened to my request, declared his enthusiastic support and said that he would talk to the right people and smooth the way for me. In actual fact he sabotaged my application.

'And later on he saw to it that all manner of difficulties were placed in my way whenever there was a question of guest performances. By that stage I was doing a lot of conducting in Italy, I'd worked in Florence and at La Scala and had many friends there. But suddenly they discovered that they were no longer able to discuss contracts with me. And the foreign section of the Reichsmusikkammer, to whom they had to apply, always turned them down whenever they asked me to work for them. They were told that I had too much to do in Berlin and had no free dates. In fact it was always Tietjen who was behind these excuses. And at that time a single statement like that from Berlin was enough, and you were more or less isolated. My contact with Tietjen, which had begun with a strange series of letters and made such a promising start in Berlin itself, had finally come to an end. We never renewed contact with each other.'

This, too, is a part of Karajan's personality. He is not interested in reconciliation, years or even decades afterwards, simply for the sake of reconciliation. Once he has a particular attitude he sticks to it, finding that there is little point in revising it simply for sentimental reasons. If he drifts apart from a colleague or if someone disappoints him, you can reckon on the situation remaining that way. Before this definitive 'breach', however, the relations between Heinz Tietjen and Herbert von Karajan were extremely fruitful, with the animosity between Tietjen and Furtwängler as the driving force: after the usual teething troubles and the serious and consistent demands that characterize all his initial encounters, Karajan had taken over the Berlin Philharmonic concerts and it was planned that he would now work closer than before with the orchestra. Furtwängler saw his position threatened, and managed to ensure that 'his' orchestra cut down the number of concerts they gave with Karajan. Tietjen saw a way out for Karajan, who was also of use to the intendant as a conductor. 'Tietjen reacted astutely. He said we should revive the traditional Sunday concerts in the State Opera – the last conductor to have given them with any success had been Erich Kleiber. Of course, I was only too pleased to agree, and it was enough for the concerts to be announced for us to be assured of success: the whole cycle was sold out within days. Of course, I had to pay a certain price for these concerts. I was now unquestionably a rival to Furtwängler and the Philharmonic, and the whole of Berlin knew it and savoured the situation.'

Karajan's relations with the Berlin Philharmonic, with whom he was later to become artistic director for life, had begun entirely according to his own prescription: they had first offered him a concert virtually without rehearsal, 'in order to get to know him', an offer which Karajan had turned down. There had then been a 'proper' concert at which Karajan had dumbfounded the orchestra and shown scant respect for its reputation by insisting upon rehearsing the string section alone before going through the programme with the whole ensemble.

'When I asked for the rehearsal, I once again heard the famous sentence, "It isn't necessary, the orchestra has the programme off pat". I still remember my reply. "They may have the programme off pat. But whether they *really* know it we'll only discover at the rehearsal. And I had a passage ready for them just before the final section of *Daphnis and Chloë*, where the strings were all over the place. We rehearsed for a whole hour on only a handful of bars. When the second group of players arrived for the later part of the rehearsal, I saw the gesture that their leader gave them: it was a raised thumb. And I knew I'd won.' Although Herbert von Karajan has promised to write about his handling of orchestras in his own book on the subject, he has no hesitation even now in revealing his patent remedy. What it comprises, in a few brief sentences, is that the conductor must see to it that an orchestral player performs all the notes in his part with the same intensity, and that he does not stop

54

playing until each individual note is actually at an end. More on this later.

Karajan's work with the Berlin Philharmonic, with whom he had already begun to make records, was interrupted first by Wilhelm Furtwängler and then by Heinz Tietjen's reaction to Furtwängler's intervention. His activities in Italy, highly successful though not yet extensive, were much curtailed by the war and by Tietjen's 'jealousy'. But the war demanded many sacrifices, and all musical activity, not only Karajan's, was considerably reduced. None the less, the conductor recalls above all 'how tremendously good it was to have got to know a musical friend like Victor De Sabata in Berlin at the right time, and how beneficial it was to be able to prepare the Sunday concerts at the State Opera in relative peace. The final terrible months in Berlin, with their bomb attacks, hunger and general uncertainty, were a marvellous time from a musical point of view.' Karajan knows very well that none of the younger generation will understand this sentence. But the sentence is correct, and all those who witnessed the end of the war will understand it correctly if they read it in context.

'Admittedly, the opera was no longer performing. But we had a whole week in which to prepare each concert. There were finally enough rehearsals, and the concerts were without exception the glorious result of intensive work. It was a terrible time, there's no question of that, but my work as a musician was almost a form of luxury for me. Of course, I was lucky, too. We were good friends of the Swiss ambassador and stayed as his guests at his castle forty kilometres outside the city, in other words, we didn't suffer so much from bomb attacks. We went to the rehearsals in the morning, and by the afternoon we were back in the glorious countryside, able to go walking for hours on end. And the concert on the Sunday was always a wonderful occasion, since the audience was literally starved of music, and so we were able to do something for them. But when "total war" was declared, and the concert halls were burned down or bombed, it was all over for us, too. Like everyone else, my wife and I just wanted to get away from Berlin.'

Although there have been no wars in our part of the world

since 1945, there is still the possibility of visiting countries where poverty or oppression or lack of freedom are rife and of seeing for oneself how concerts become much more than just musical events. If Karajan describes the final wartime concerts he gave in Berlin as though they were the best he can remember, he does not mean it in a purely musical sense. What he remembers is the unrepeatable experience of performing for a starving public that was also starved of music. None the less, he passes quickly over this period, too, and turns the final days of the war, which he did not have to spend in Berlin, into a brief chapter of its own, a kind of episode which he had to get through in order to reach the most important period of his life.

'In order to travel abroad at that time, what you needed above all was an official invitation. I asked my friends in Italy to get me one – it was intended merely to be a conducting engagement. A formality, simply to have a guarantee of work outside Berlin. It finally worked, and I received an invitation to give several radio concerts in Milan, together with the necessary visa. In Italy, of course, there was no longer any thought of organizing radio concerts. The war was already much too close, they really had other worries. However, we stayed in a hotel, we had the chance to go out to eat, we were no longer living in the midst of terror. There was a sort of apocalyptic mood. Everyone knew that the foreign troops were advancing and tried to persuade us to get to Switzerland as quickly as possible. But no one could say how we could have got to Switzerland. And when it became dangerous for Germans like us to remain in Milan, friends of ours invited us to stay with them in Como. Their villa was already full, family relatives were waiting in all the rooms for the war to end. But they had room for us in their boathouse, and so we lived right by the lake, the boats rocked gently to and fro beneath us, and we thought we'd never be found.'

As for the end of the war and the period that followed, Karajan's account is briefer than his admirers, fond of detail as they are, would no doubt wish.

'But it was clear that not even in Como could we remain undetected. It was while I was here that I received my call-up papers. At the very last minute they wanted me in the army. I had to see the general, who explained to me that he had to send me back to Berlin. But he looked at me very calmly and said he'd first have to find a place in an aeroplane for me, and that could take some time. Nothing could be done for two weeks at the soonest, but I was to remain on stand-by during that period – and I realized then that he would not find a free seat for me. And so it was. Years later I met him again, when I was taking the Vienna Symphony Orchestra on our first tour of Germany. After one of the concerts he was waiting for me in the foyer; he came up to me and explained that he had only wanted to see that all was going well for me . . . He may have saved my life in 1945, there's no knowing what might have happened if I had had to return to Berlin at the last minute. But at that time, when my call-up papers arrived and also my temporary rescue, I swore I'd withdraw into myself for the coming period: "You won't complain, you won't justify yourself, you'll simply remain calm and wait for the time when you can work once again as a completely free person." I resolved to do so, and I kept my word. I did not get involved in the whole rigmarole that went on at the end of the war and during the period that followed. I remained perfectly calm – and throughout this period, although it was a bad time for me, I benefited from my decision.'

After the Second World War

'We survived the end of the war and the days that followed with a lawyer in Milan – we'd gone to see him about our future, but he simply told us we couldn't leave his house, otherwise our lives would be in danger. And so we stayed with him for two weeks. Even today I don't know how to thank him. He saved us.

'We then moved into a dreadful little hotel, with a window looking out on to a fire wall. We'd no money, and no chance of earning any. And, of course, we'd no contacts with the outside world. It was the worst time of my life – but it was also the moment I learned Italian. I spent our last remaining money on German and Italian books, drew up a timetable to which I stuck with iron resolve, was my own teacher and ensured that, as pupil, I maintained a strict sense of discipline. And by the time we were finally able to go out into the street, I had complete mastery of Italian, I could not only read it, I could also speak it. And so even this dreadful time was not without a purpose: I can always find a sense of purpose whenever I look back on any period in my life. It was terrible and painful to be condemned to doing nothing, not to be able to perform music. And it was a matter of immense importance to me to speak good Italian. It was an ability I was able to put to good use later on.

'Of course, I tried to conduct again, in spite of everything. But it was no good. In Milan, where I still had a certain reputation, there was no thought of allowing me to appear. The Americans said that enquiries would first have to be made regarding my person, and in any case everyone had their own worries. But then an old English friend of mine suddenly turned up, an officer in the British occupying forces who was stationed in Trieste. He had heard I was in Italy and so he invited me to

Trieste. In Trieste there was nothing the Americans could say –
I was invited, we drove to Trieste, the promised concert turned
into three concerts, it was a good start. They also promised to
send me across the border into Austria. But nothing came of
that for the time being. No means of transporting civilians . . .

'Until my knowledge of foreign languages finally proved of
use. I was asked to act as translator for a party of refugees who
were being transported to Austria. In return we had to spend a
week in a refugee camp: it was dreadful, the surroundings, the
hunger, the hopelessness. But it was also a chance to get home.

'The train journey from Trieste to Klagenfurt took twenty-nine
hours. You can't imagine what it was like to travel by train at
that time, and how happy you were to be travelling by train at
all. But after twenty-nine hours we arrived in Klagenfurt. And
found a way of getting to Salzburg. And so, in one way and
another, we finally arrived home.

'To begin with, I stayed in my parents' home, after which
we retired to the country. I took my scores with me and buried
myself in music, following the same sort of timetable that I had
adopted when learning Italian. I studied new music, but I also
worked through all the pieces that I had been conducting for
years. There was little to eat, and no one to look after you.
But there were my scores, there was music, and by the time
this period, too, was over, I was better and more adequately
prepared for my future commitments than ever before.'

There is no doubt that Herbert von Karajan has really been
speaking here on the subject of self-discipline. I know of no
one more qualified to speak on the topic than he is. He never
discusses the factor that triggers off such a 'test', he simply
explains how to survive it. By setting oneself a challenge and
sticking at it. When it is all over – and in life everything comes
to an end sooner or later – you feel you've achieved something
and that you've benefited from it. At least that is what Karajan
claims and proves by his own example. First, because you have
not given up, and, second, because you have gained from what
you've been through. Gained knowledge and insights.

Just as he broaches this subject concisely and unpretentiously,
so he speaks briefly and unaccusingly about the time when

60

he was 'banned', when many of his colleagues invested their energies in attempting to relaunch their careers with all due despatch. 'For me the question whether this enforced break was a kind of penance simply does not arise.' All too conscious of the fact that there are many readers who want to gain a more intimate understanding not only of Karajan the musician but also of Karajan the man, I knew that questions on the conductor's situation after 1945 could simply not be avoided. But they had to be asked in a way that was neither probing nor painful. Karajan answered them in his typically brisk and precise manner, as though it were the most natural thing in the world. After all, he had lived with these questions for forty years.

'I was of the view that certain courts were preparing to act which had no right to pass judgement on me. There had been a war over which no one could simply pass sentence. And those people whose job it was to decide whether I should conduct or not – these were people I knew too much about to be able to acknowledge them as competent authorities. I knew something about their private occupations. I saw how they behaved. I didn't want their mercy, which they were constantly being begged to show. I knew it was simply a time of transition. I knew that there would be a law one day. And that I'd be able to work again. And so I simply refused to play along.

'And today I think I acted correctly. For what emerged from all those interrogations and highly incompetent commissions? Justice? Truth? Did these investigations really bring anything to light? Who benefited from them? Documents were produced and statements from witnesses were used as evidence. And there were documents and witnesses for the other side. In almost every instance lies were told – that, at least, can be proved today, for the sentences which were passed at that time have all been shown to be untenable. It would have been wrong, I thought at the time, to appear before a tribunal and claim one was totally innocent. But, of course, the opposite was also totally wrong and senseless.

'I still remember the American theatre officer – he was called Peter Passetti – sending for me and asking why I had not been to see him to apply for permission to perform in public. I do not know whether he interpreted my attitude correctly, whether he understood why I had not come cap in hand and taken up residence in his waiting room. But for me my attitude was the only possible way of surviving that period. I remained silent and busied myself with music. And when it came to my first concert in Vienna, I was older and wiser than before, and my first appearance with the Vienna Philharmonic turned out to be a wonderful occasion.'

The first invitation to conduct a concert came from Vienna. The concert was fixed for January 1946. If the ban on Karajan had lasted only six brief months, his attitude would have been easily understandable. But his first concert in the Grosser Musikvereinssaal was far from marking the end of that period. The ban had only been temporarily lifted . . .

Immediately before the concert Karajan and the first violinist of the orchestra had to go to the Hotel Imperial. The hotel is situated between the Musikverein and the Ringstrasse, and at the time in question was the headquarters of the Soviet occupying forces. Fritz Sedlak, the first violinist and leader of a famous string quartet, had learned Russian as a prisoner-of-war during the First World War, and the orchestra benefited from his linguistic expertise. The Vienna Philharmonic has always made a point of using its members' abilities for mutual benefit.

'We arrived at the hotel, or rather the headquarters, at nine o'clock in the morning. The interview lasted until one. Of course, it wasn't so much an interview as an interrogation. It was my past they wanted to know about. Nazi or non-Nazi? The officer spoke without a break; Sedlak answered, without consulting me. I simply sat there and occasionally discovered what exactly they were discussing. I had no way of contributing anything to the interview. And at one o'clock Sedlak finally said what I'd been waiting for him to say all morning, "I must point out that we need your decision now. Will the concert take place in two hours from now or not? If we have to cancel, we'll have to put up notices on the door and give people their money back." To which the officer said only one word, "Yes". Sedlak had won, the concert could go ahead. I just had time to change when I got to the Musikverein.

'It was a wonderful concert, we performed a symphony by

Haydn, *Don Juan* by Richard Strauss and Brahms's First Symphony. But – it was the only concert. Although a second one was announced at once, it was cancelled by the Russians. No explanation was given for the ban, there were only rumours of the kind that were common in the Vienna of that time. The occupying powers were said not to have reached agreement at one of their joint sessions on some important, in other words, non-cultural matter. When they finally did get round to discussing culture, the representative of the American occupying forces mentioned my name, and the representative of the Soviet occupying forces answered with an angry "Nyet". My "case" was certainly not on the agenda, it was not discussed, and I was banned because of a single word on the fringes of a meeting. The Philharmonic, who had to cancel their concert at the last minute, were stunned. They sent Sedlak to see me again, but he told me he really didn't know what the best course of action was. For my own part, I told the orchestra, "Don't worry. We shall play together on many occasions in future." '

A further round of music, politics and confrontation followed, which Herbert von Karajan remembers not least because it brought him together, once and for all, with Vienna and the Gesellschaft der Musikfreunde. He was appointed their artistic director for life, a link which he emphasizes at every opportunity. Their way of thanking him is to ignore all the discussions that have taken place around Karajan during recent decades, and loyally and gratefully to set store by meeting his wishes and acknowledging him as the ultimate authority on each and every question. The two presidents and two general secretaries who have run the Gesellschaft der Musikfreunde since the end of the Second World War have been Karajan's most faithful friends in every situation. And Karajan rewards such loyalty.

'In fact it was not long before we were performing together again, this time a benefit performance for the Philharmonic, although the general public were excluded. For my first concert Walter Legge of Columbia Records had come to Vienna. He wanted to make gramophone recordings with us and discovered all kinds of special provisions to make it possible. His company was not allowed at that time to sign contracts with Austrians.

And so they founded their own branch offices in Switzerland and in that way were able to sign up the Vienna Philharmonic and me. As you can imagine, it meant not only the pleasure of performing together but also our first financial guarantee – in Swiss francs. We worked a great deal together, always in earnest, arranged our recording dates around the Philharmonic's other commitments and, whenever possible, were in front of microphones in the Grosser Musikvereinssaal.

'To begin with, however, it looked as though the Legge project would come to nothing: the British occupying forces protested. So the then President of the Gesellschaft der Musikfreunde, Alexander Hryntschak, intervened and declared that not even the occupying powers could pronounce any further bans. He said very clearly, "You can ban Herbert von Karajan from appearing in public. But what we do in our own house is entirely our own affair and does not come under your jurisdiction. Nor can you prevent Herr von Karajan from sitting in our director's box in future, since he is our artistic head."

'It required courage at that time to say such things, and a very personal, brave approach. President Hryntschak died long ago, but I never forgot his courage, and I shall never forget the Gesellschaft der Musikfreunde for electing me their concert director for life in 1947, at what was still a very critical time. It's a unique position. Before me, the concert directors were Herbeck, Richter, Hellmesberger and Johannes Brahms. In the musical city of Vienna it's a position you can be proud of all your life.'

Some of the interviews which made this book possible took place in fact in the Musikverein building overlooking the Karlsplatz in Vienna. On the ground floor, right next to the board room, there is another room still known as the 'boss's room'. It is small and unprepossessing and, apart from a piano, it has only a bench and an armchair brought out of store: the former general secretary Rudolf Gamsjäger had these pieces of furniture removed from his office and left here when he himself had no further use for them. Occasional visitors who come here expecting to find a breath of luxury not just in the most venerable of all Vienna's musical institutions but, more especially, in the official office of Herbert von Karajan are deeply shocked. But that's not Herbert von Karajan. Although he has spent the greater part of his working life in the greatest and, no doubt, the wealthiest opera houses and concert halls in the world, he has never set store by personal luxury. Wherever you track him down, you will find him in extremely unpretentious surroundings and sense his total disinterest in ostentation. He has never received his interviewers or other negotiating parties with any degree of extravagance, and has never outgrown the improvised furnishings in rooms which he has been using since the earliest post-war period. His piano must be well tuned, and he and his interviewer must each have an armchair at their disposal. That is all that Herbert von Karajan ever wants.

This seems to me to be characteristic of an artist who, time and again, is described as 'insanely expensive' and who has had to put up with being reckoned among the international jet set: of all the directors and maestri it has been my privilege to know, he is the only one who finds status symbols repugnant. The only one for whom a special artist's room has not had to be made ready in any concert hall. The only one who, still mindful of the difficult times he lived through in the Musikverein, would describe it as senseless expense to refurnish his room. He values comfort and knows that certain qualities are necessary to be able to work. But in this context luxury is of no meaning to him.

When he recalls the 'old days' at the Musikverein, it is to evoke pictures of endless rehearsals with the Singverein and the long period that he spent working with the Vienna Symphonic. And, of course, Wilhelm Furtwängler, who was also staying in Vienna during the post-war period. 'I was already concert director when Furtwängler conducted his first Philharmonic concert after the war. I'll never forget him waiting in the green room before the concert. Demonstrations had been announced, and someone in the auditorium did actually get up to protest at Furtwängler's presence. There followed all the expected protests, and Furtwängler, who was always a very insecure person, simply did not know how to react. I told him, "Dr Furtwängler, don't take it seriously. Go to the podium and conduct. And then they'll all stop protesting."'

Karajan had also been taken on as artistic adviser to the

Salzburg Festival, and, although he himself was prevented from conducting, he was willing, in the name of the Festival, to persuade Furtwängler to appear in Salzburg, too. 'He really was an extremely irresolute person. He never knew what he should say to my insistent request. I asked for his definite agreement. But he left everything in the air. I tried again during the winter of 1947. I was on the Arlberg and discovered that Furtwängler was on his way to Zurich. And so I telephoned and asked him at least to give me a hearing on his journey through the Arlberg and finally come to a decision. It really was the middle of winter. We talked and talked, and Furtwängler proved as indecisive as ever. When he asked what opera he was being offered in Salzburg and I said *Fidelio*, he was finally won over and agreed. I remember this journey and the conversation very well, because I got out of the train and walked back home from Stuben over the Arlberg. I became caught up in a blizzard and could only get my bearings from the posts at the side of the road. But one of the posts must have been badly marked, because I wandered away from the road and almost lost my way. By the time I found the road again, it was to be met by members of a search party who had been sent out to look for me. If I'd not been in training then and if I'd not also been very lucky, I could have frozen to death winning back Wilhelm Furtwängler for the Salzburg Festival.'

It is almost in passing that Karajan remembers these stories, however much they are part and parcel of his curious relationship with his once great rival. After decades in which this rivalry has been the subject of endless discussion and during which Karajan himself has refused to comment, there is now a slightly ironic, even sentimental tinge to his voice when he talks about Furtwängler. He tells stories which prove that he has a different assessment of Furtwängler as both conductor and man than his fanatical admirers. But it does not occur to him to speak dismissively of an important colleague from a time which, he thinks, drew to an irrevocable close with Furtwängler's death. You can sense a great deal of feeling when Karajan talks about Furtwängler. At least that is true in 1987, when books are still being written that seek to revive old grudges. Karajan does not give way to these wishes. There is no point expecting him to contribute to the subject.

Although it is possible to understand the situation, Herbert von Karajan's attitude seems to have been one of reserve towards the conductor whom he thought of, to the very end, clearly as an obstacle. Karajan admits that he never found it possible to have a proper conversation with Furtwängler, and, of course, he does not forget that even after the war barriers kept coming down whenever he strayed into an area which had been regarded as Furtwängler's domain. Although it was Karajan himself who lured Furtwängler back to Salzburg, he found, after the initial post-war festivals, that there were suddenly no longer any opera productions for him to conduct. Only after Furtwängler's death was Karajan summoned back to his home town, a town where he has remained, so to speak, ever since. Even the Vienna Philharmonic bowed to the demands of their chief conductor Wilhelm Furtwängler and for a long time refused to give concerts with Karajan. The latter drew his own conclusions and worked so intensively with the Vienna Symphonic that the period under him, with a Karajan cycle at the Musikverein and a series of major invitations to tour abroad, was without doubt the most successful in the orchestra's history.

At rehearsals, or in conversation with groups of people, Karajan restricts himself to telling minor anecdotes about his great adversary. When a more serious note creeps into his reminiscences, he none the less remains reserved and polite towards the memory of a musician whose interpretative genius he never calls into doubt.

'We met in Salzburg during the summer. Furtwängler was staying at a small hotel above the Mozart Cinema in the Kaigasse. I remember a meal we had together. It passed off very formally. Only when I made a joke at the expense of another conductor did Furtwängler laugh his booming laugh and seem in a better mood. But there was no real basis for conversation there. After all, I discovered that he was asking openly in Salzburg, "Does Karajan always have to conduct here?" The following summer he took over two operas, and the summer after that he even had three opera productions, by which time there was nothing left for me any longer.

'But these are memories of a time which is long since past. Past and forgotten. And Furtwängler was a relatively insecure person in almost everything. For example, he never stopped worrying about his concert programmes and wondering whether he should change them. It reached the point where it was impossible to have any posters printed and the programmes were never ready in time. I know Rudolf Effenberger, the legendary custodian of the green room at the Musikverein, once said to him, "Look, Dr Furtwängler, why are you getting so worked up? From now on let's simply do as follows: you'll come to the green room before each concert and tell me what you want to play. I'll then go out on to the platform and tell the audience. That will satisfy everyone." And, of course, it was just the same in Salzburg. Whenever a new programme was put together, he would worry about what the clergy would say. For a long time I didn't understand his concern. After all, why should the Salzburg clergy burden itself with worries about the Festival's concert programmes? But that's how Furtwängler was; his many letters and essays prove after all that he really didn't make life easy for himself.

'In spite of our confrontations I still think very highly of him. As a musician there is a great deal I have to thank him for – I heard him rehearsing and performing and learned a tremendous amount by doing so. Later on, I had a lot to do with many of the orchestras that had passed through his school – they were not only excellent musicians, they also talked about Furtwängler with me and admitted that I'd always judged him correctly as a musician. It was always my wish to keep alive that aspect of his own artistry that I found especially great, and transfer it to my own concerts, and I believe that, to a certain extent, I have succeeded in doing so.

'The suggestion that, as the younger of us, I was for ever upsetting him through the very fact of my existence is not one to be taken seriously. It was always easy to upset Furtwängler. I remember that he once declared that he could not conduct one of the Musikverein concerts – it was simply too much for him to conduct a programme on four consecutive evenings. The general

68

secretary attempted to salvage at least two of the concerts, and Furtwängler agreed to think about it. And, as always, he left the matter unresolved. Time was pressing, Gamsjäger got on the telephone and, after trying a considerable number of conductors, finally came up with Eugen Jochum, who was free on the dates in question. Jochum promised to take over the concerts, the posters were ordered, the proof copy arrived in the building and was placed on the secretary's desk. And Furtwängler came along, saw the draft poster and said very, very reproachfully, "Well, that didn't take long". He simply didn't understand that the concerts couldn't be cancelled. He didn't understand that they had to look for another conductor for the concerts. He was only very annoyed that they'd looked round for a replacement following his refusal to conduct.'

Karajan freely admits that Wilhelm Furtwängler's rivalry was of benefit to him – it drove him abroad at just the right time and brought him into contact with orchestras elsewhere. With the orchestra, for example, that Walter Legge was creating in London, chiefly in order to be able to produce more records. 'Legge had been preparing for this orchestra even while the war was still on. In England it was the case that any orchestral player who was on leave from the front had to report for duty and make himself available to give concerts. Concerts were arranged throughout the war, Sunday after Sunday, the ensemble was for ever changing, but they achieved an extremely high standard with only a few rehearsals – and Walter Legge was able to take notes and mark down the best players for the period when the war was over. He was one of the organizers of these concerts, and he felt very much that it was a British speciality to be able to sight-read even works of a high degree of difficulty – and he completed his list. By the end of the war he immediately produced an apparently perfect ensemble that only required organizing.

'When Legge invited me to help him build up the orchestra, I saw it as a particularly interesting challenge. It was a question of beginning at the very beginning, so to speak. There was not even a name for the ensemble, though we had fourteen ex-leaders all engaged as first violins. It's true! They really all had been leaders of various orchestras in their time, but they all wanted to remain in London. There were also a couple of Americans, who didn't want to return to the States.

'Of course, everyone thinks to begin with that such a high standard of technique is a blessing in terms of orchestral quality. But we soon sensed that it was causing a particular problem: a violinist who has once been leader of an orchestra will have acquired quite special qualities of leadership which he cannot get rid of. It is virtually impossible for him to sit at the third or fourth desk and allow himself to be led by a colleague. What attracted me to this job was that I could achieve a degree of ensemble playing with these musicians that was more than merely the result of a machine in perfect working order.

'The Philharmonia Orchestra was technically perfect from the word go. I remember having doubts on the way to the first rehearsal – we were to do *Rosenkavalier*, and I couldn't imagine it going at all well. Legge reassured me, and he was right to do so. We began with the prelude, and from that moment onwards there was no longer any need to stop even once. On the other hand, the orchestra had its limitations which it was unable to transcend – limitations which made my departure easier when it came. Once a work had been rehearsed with the players, you knew exactly what it would sound like at the concert. Once a certain standard had been achieved, it was always repeated, you could rely on it. But you couldn't expect the players to improve at a concert. That would simply have been inconsistent with their understanding.

'I know now of a good comparison: the London players were just like a youth orchestra. You can have wonderful rehearsal sessions with them, all young musicians are fully conversant with their instruments and passionately committed to what they are doing. But at the evening's concert they play with exactly the same enthusiasm as at the rehearsal – they're not yet capable of outstripping themselves. I know what I'm talking about, since the Philharmonic players in Berlin and Vienna are the exact and glorious opposite. Our rehearsals together are wonderful, but at the concert in the evening there is always something extra that I could not hear and could not sense at the rehearsal. They then play with precisely those nuances which I never heard in London.

'Even so, the work in London kept me fascinated for a long time. We produced one recording after another, we went on tour – and finally we drifted apart. It expressed itself in petty reproaches on the part of the players, who said that at the end of a concert I didn't return to the platform often enough to take a bow, and that I was undermining the orchestra's successes . . . I simply didn't understand these reproaches, what interested me was the rehearsals and the performances, not unleashing torrents of applause after a concert. But there were also more important reasons why I finally parted company with the London orchestra: I received invitations from the Salzburg Festival, the Vienna State Opera and the Berlin Philharmonic. Walter Legge asked me what I really wanted. And I told him that I wanted an orchestra that was like a wall I could always lean against. Legge knew that that was something he couldn't offer me. We went our separate ways but remained friends. I had benefited a great deal from him and his orchestra, that's undeniable.'

It was during a tour with the Philharmonia Orchestra and Clara Haskil that Karajan received the first cautious, then more determined, approach from Salzburg. First, it was one opera that was discussed, then several operas, until finally Oscar Fritz Schuh and the Festival president Baron Puthon explained what they really wanted to know: they wanted him to become the Festival's artistic director but were afraid that they would be taking on a 'dictator'. When Karajan tells this story, he is forced to laugh, even if only to himself. 'My answer to this question was quickly given. "I shall be a dictator." I knew the situation in Salzburg. The programme was approved by a board of directors. And, of course, they wanted things to remain as they were. I was in favour of an alternative plan of a kind that has always worked in practice in Salzburg: I wanted to submit a plan for the coming season and have it approved by the board of directors. That's how it had been in fact under Bruno Walter, Arturo Toscanini and finally under Wilhelm Furtwängler. And to begin with it worked with me, as well. Until the Grosses Festspielhaus was opened there were virtually no problems – I finally resigned from the position because I didn't want to be bothered with the details of planning a festival and because I began to sense

71

how the general public was judging the situation. Everything that was good and successful about Salzburg was said to be a success for the Festival, but when things didn't work, it was me who was blamed. Basically nothing has changed here right down to the present day. There is a board of directors, I am a member of that board, and whenever anything happens in Salzburg, they can use me as an excuse, as indeed they do. I can scarcely remember a single occasion when I've been credited with sound decisions that have been taken by the board of directors.'

Looked at more closely, the Salzburg Festival has in fact changed a great deal. And it is Herbert von Karajan who has increased his commitment to the way the Festival is run, insisting on convening more and more board meetings and demanding information about individual artists' engagements or other contractual details. He himself does not say as much, but this seems to be his entirely personal approach to the responsibility that is heaped upon him: he takes it on wholeheartedly. And he takes it with all its necessary implications. What this means is that at times when the general public is debating the state of his health, Karajan himself is heading a delegation to the newly appointed Minister for the Arts, explaining to her the Festival's financial needs and the consequences that would follow if the Festival budget were cut back. No one reads about this meeting, there are no sensational interviews, but the Salzburg Festival receives the necessary approval for a subsidy for the coming years, a sum identical to that which the board of directors had reckoned was necessary for the Festival's future survival. Herbert von Karajan was officially in Vienna for rehearsals and concert performances, that's all that the general public learns, all that Herbert von Karajan himself wishes to be known. That he has invested his energies in budgetary discussions is simply another of his jobs as a member of the Festival committee.

For those who are enamoured of precise dates there are several anthologies dealing with Karajan's activities. As far as the present volume is concerned, it will be clear on closer examination that it is the important dates which it does not occur to Herbert von Karajan to mention. It is not that he has forgotten them, but because, for him, they belong only to the past. The time when he went on tour with the Philharmonia Orchestra was also the time when he renewed his links with Berlin and Vienna, but above all the time when he worked at La Scala, Milan, and gained a reputation which he had not previously had as a conductor with authentic links with Italian grand opera and great Italian interpreters. Karajan had met Victor De Sabata during the war and even today speaks fulsomely of the musicality and astonishing musical memory of a colleague who remained loyal in his friendship even in the post-war years. They met again in Milan, where Karajan admired De Sabata's performances of German music even more than the *italianità* which he imbibed at source, working closely with the singers and musicians at La Scala.

Even before he took up his so-called leading appointments, Karajan had travelled widely, he had conducted throughout the world and left his traces wherever he went. But when it finally comes to it, there *is* a date which Herbert von Karajan still remembers, even today. 'We were in Italy when news of Furtwängler's death arrived. To begin with, it was an anonymous telegram, then I read the newspapers, and then came the first approaches from the Berlin Philharmonic who were supposed to be going on tour to America with Furtwängler.

'And at the same time there was a telephone call from New York. The impresario of an American concert agency gave me to understand that he was expecting me to conduct this tour. He was prepared to call off the tour if he couldn't have me and the Berlin Philharmonic. But I still had my contract with La Scala and had to explain to my friend Ghiringhelli that I would either rehearse *The Valkyrie* with him or go to Berlin and take charge there. I spoke very frankly with him and told him I was leaving the decision to him, but that I'd remain in Milan if he insisted. But Ghiringhelli said that he understood exactly what the Berlin offer meant to me, and he released me from my contract, something I've never forgotten.

'Then came the period of negotiations in Berlin. I had explained to the orchestra's representatives that I would go to America with the Philharmonic only as Furtwängler's successor designate, and they confirmed that that would be so. That was enough for me, but it was wrong, as I now know. I ought to have insisted on immediate confirmation and not got involved in lengthy negotiations. But I was overjoyed, too intoxicated by the idea of conducting this splendid orchestra. I began rehearsing with them in Berlin, more and more days went by, and still there was no contract. When, on the eleventh day, I finally asked where the contract was, they invented various excuses. One of the senators whose signature was needed for the contract was ill, another was out of town. I suddenly sensed that things would not go entirely my own way.

'And so I went to see the mayor and explained my problem to him: they had begun by promising me everything I wanted, but now they suddenly preferred to take me on a trial basis. Under the circumstances I would not feel happy on tour. Not for nothing was the mayor a leading politician. He understood the situation immediately and asked with a laugh what could be done. I made a suggestion, and he accepted it. He gave a press conference at which I was asked, publicly, whether I would be prepared to accept the post of artistic director of the Berlin Philharmonic on our return from the tour. My answer to Reuter's question became proverbial: 'with immense pleasure.' It was under these auspices that we set off on our first tour together. It meant that the whole affair was now settled for me.'

But it wasn't, as Herbert von Karajan now explains decades later, fully conscious of the fact that, although they have had great times together, he has also had a phenomenal row with the orchestra. In 1987 there are no longer any discussions, the Berlin Philharmonic has come to terms with the reality of the situation and is again Karajan's orchestra. In the intervening period they had exchanged formal notes and had been made to realize that Karajan could release them from their commitments, while they in turn had tried to get out of their contractual obligations. Public interest in these disagreements was intense and neither the conductor nor the orchestra met with universal approval – it was all too clear that artistic and commercial questions were too closely bound up with each other and that, by the time they had declared their willingness to co-operate with their conductor for life, the Berlin Philharmonic had weighed up the artistic and commercial aspects extremely closely.

Karajan, however, sees the roots of this much later discord in the earliest negotiations surrounding his contract. 'I did not receive my contract on our return from America, but not until two years later. They made a fuss over the term "for life" and declared that such a formula could not be used in a contract. So I told them they could draw up a contract specifying a term of ninety years. Finally, the lawyers came to see me and said that I'd receive exactly the same contract that Furtwängler had had. But that was not entirely true. It was a question of ensuring that the orchestra's manager be appointed and dismissed by the mayor in agreement with their artistic director. What it actually says in my contract – which I did not discover until years later – was not "agreement" but "consultation", which means virtually nothing. Only that I have to be informed. When they finally told me, I was scandalized. It means, as I told them, that my contract is no more than a scrap of paper that they can do with whatever they want. They simply lied to me at the time.

'It is now far too late to discuss it all over again, even if there were any point in doing so. I wanted to have this orchestra at any price because I was fascinated by its qualities and because I knew what I could achieve with it. There was only one reason why I was attached to the idea of a contract for life, and that was because I wanted the orchestra to have plenty of time for us all to become of one mind. I wanted to ensure in advance that no newly elected senator could come along and put an end to our work together. And our common development has proved me right. The orchestra and I have been together now for three generations of players, and it is only this sense of community over several decades that has made us so great. On one occasion, when we were at loggerheads, I said loudly and clearly in Berlin that an act of deception had been committed at the very outset of negotiations. But I also have to say that, throughout the decades, the orchestra has been exactly what I dreamed it would be. It was the wall behind me on which I can still lean, even now.'

The reader must bear in mind that Herbert von Karajan's observations concerning his work together with various ensembles are characterized by the fact that all the complicated links.

which once bound him to institutions throughout the world are now as good as severed. Karajan has shown remarkable consistency of purpose in this respect, concentrating his field of operations whenever the opportunity has presented itself, and, far from expanding his activities, reducing them in scope. And he has done so, moreover, not when operations and illnesses would otherwise have forced him to abandon his whistle-stop tours and flying visits, but, so to speak, at the height of his 'power' (although he himself never uses such a word). Karajan himself never fails to remind his listener that it is decades since he last conducted a 'foreign' orchestra. 'I realized one day that the effort required to establish a high-voltage relationship with each new ensemble was no longer worth the while. I knew that the time when I could work together with several different ensembles was finally over. I had had many wonderful experiences, and I know that even today I could of course quickly resume working with a good orchestra – I could certainly perform well with any of them. But I cut short this development of my own accord, and the state of my health and the need to realize my own plans now make it out of the question. Perhaps I'd like to conduct the Leningrad Philharmonic again, I'm sure we'd work together splendidly. But I cannot see any free time in my diary.'

One does not sense any great resignation in such considerations. But then resignation is not a characteristic tone for Karajan to adopt. Even on days when he needs a great deal of self-discipline before he can force himself to conduct an interview or work on his music films, the impression he makes is anything other than one of resignation. He seems very purposeful, very concentrated, very much concerned to make the best of his condition and at least to attempt to make some progress, however effortful such progress may be.

His interviewer must repeat once again that Herbert von Karajan clearly has an inexhaustible supply of willpower. And this willpower is directed towards a single goal, the most perfect possible record of his central repertory in terms of concerts, records and films, a repertory which Karajan intends shall preserve something that he believes today's leading conductors have already lost. Time and again Karajan says that he sees himself as the last of the old kapellmeisters. Time and again he implies that he wants to hand on and preserve an aspect of music which will no longer exist when he puts away his baton for the last time. Time and again he admits of course that even then there will still be music and still be musicians, and that he is conscious of a continuing development. And time and again he declines to pass judgement or make disparaging remarks about what will come after him.

It will be different, and everyone who sees and hears his musical testament will be able to tell the difference.

'For me the process represented by conducting remains as fascinating as ever, involving as it does the transference of one person's individual will on to an orchestra. But it is a self-contained chapter in my life which I no longer need to experience. If I now know that I would get along famously with those Russian musicians, I also recall how quickly I found the right rapport with American musicians. I once conducted the Cleveland Orchestra at the Salzburg Festival. That was in George Szell's day, a man I admired greatly both as a musician and as an orchestral conductor. He had the reputation of being unpleasant and sarcastic as a boss, and it was said that his orchestra suffered a lot from his spiteful remarks – but I knew him only as a charming and pleasant individual. I only know that, half an hour before the first orchestra rehearsal was due to start in Salzburg, he invited me to talk with him. We chatted about trivialities. Only later did I realize that, having trained his orchestra to be extremely punctual, he wanted to be sure that I would make a good, punctual impression on them. And immediately before the concert he called the cello section of the orchestra to a special rehearsal which I really wouldn't have considered necessary, but he wanted his players to make the very best impression on me. He also confessed to me, "I thought it would be a catastrophe. Your own intentions are diametrically opposed to the ones I have with the orchestra. But after twenty minutes I'd got over my shock. The orchestra in fact played for you exactly the opposite of what I normally ask of them."'

And when, as so rarely happens, Karajan names individual names, describing George Szell as a good conductor and enthusing over Victor De Sabata, then you understand what he means when he says he would always like to have been a synthesis of Furtwängler and Toscanini.

'There is one respect in which I feel myself to be Furtwängler's legitimate successor. Whenever he conducted a concert he would repeatedly leave the orchestra to get on without him. During transitional passages he would consciously hesitate to take the lead, letting the players feel that it was they whom he wanted to place the next chord, and so he waited: the Berliners still tell me of the apparently helpless expression with which he looked at the orchestra and waited for them to continue on their own. And they continued playing for him.

'But there is no sense in giving an orchestra total freedom. Just as there is no sense in being over-explicit in showing them where I'd like to go slower, for example. The players can sense what is going to happen. I myself have a tempo in my head long before I come to the passage in question. I know in advance, so to speak, what is going to happen. And the players react faultlessly, they don't need a gesture or a glance from me.

'By contrast, I can also tell in advance when something is going to go wrong in the orchestra. I really can sense in advance if a player has problems with his breathing, and so I'll go faster for him. I sense in advance the fear that a player feels at a difficult entry, and I help him so that we get over the passage quickly together. Time and again the players come up to me after a concert and confirm that there was a tricky passage – but the concert is long since over, we mastered the problem together and in retrospect share the feeling that the day has again been saved.'

And Toscanini? 'He was in fact exactly the opposite in the way he conducted. I often watched him and finally realized at what point in his rehearsals the difficulties that were often associated with him began: it was only in works which he loved above all else. If he was rehearsing a Rossini overture, he simply played it through. As music it was so self-evident to him that the orchestra realized at once what he wanted. But when he rehearsed Debussy, for example, there were always the most almighty rows. I think he had a tonal image of *La Mer*, for example, which was simply not realizable. And I understand him, since I, too, find it difficult to hear what I'd like to hear in this work. Sometimes I think we are all looking for something in this piece that Debussy simply did not write. But the really major problems that Toscanini encountered at rehearsals always arose when Beethoven was on the programme. He was always in despair – and all because of his love of Beethoven. I know of one rehearsal in Vienna when Toscanini began to work through his usual repertoire of enraged reactions, throwing the score to the ground, smashing his watch and swearing at the orchestra. The Philharmonic players knew what was coming and were prepared for it. So that when Toscanini tried to go one better and abandon the rehearsal, he found that the orchestra had locked both the doors leading away from the platform. When he tried to get out of the hall and found himself standing in front of the locked doors, he realized that his outburst of anger had been anticipated. For a few minutes he went and stood in a corner, like a small child, and was ashamed of what he had done. He then returned to his music stand and wasted no more words on the situation, but continued with the rehearsal. But the Vienna Philharmonic had an additional joke to tell about this rehearsal: they bought a ticket in the local lottery on the basis of the page numbers in the score at the point where the interruption had taken place, and they won what, for the time, was a considerable sum of money. They told Toscanini, who reacted, surprisingly, by doubling the winnings out of his own fee. I particularly like this story because it says so much about Toscanini both as a man and as a musician. He was anything but ill-tempered. His outbursts were always because he could not bear not to hear the music he had imagined. At such moments he was genuinely and sincerely offended and so he screamed at the players. With his threatening gestures and his sure-fire beat he was the exact opposite of Wilhelm Furtwängler, the great vacillator.

'All the orchestras who worked with Toscanini benefited enormously from his way of conducting. And Furtwängler's request to his players that they free him from his predicament and play on also left a deep and lasting impression on the Philharmonic orchestras in Berlin and Vienna. It was my dream to combine the aims of both these conductors. As I said many years ago by way of a joke, you can get an orchestra to the point where the violinists will even hold their right feet in exactly the way the conductor tells them to, but at the same time it is also possible for these same violinists, after many rehearsals together, suddenly to give more at a concert than had ever been demanded of them at a rehearsal. Something, moreover, that you only dream of during the performance.'

Elsewhere – as we shall see – Karajan describes his own way of rehearsing. And he gives at least in part his, so to speak, extremely simple 'prescriptions' for the orchestral sound he would like to have and which, as even his most critical listeners will concede, he always gets exactly as he wants. But here his memories are of a time when he was boss in Salzburg and Berlin and about to become boss in Vienna, so that it is important for him here to speak only of his orchestras and of the way he concentrated on them. It is at this point that it occurs to his interviewer how impossible it is to persuade the Austrian conductor from Salzburg to admit his nationality. Of course, his intonation and disposition are Austrian, while his knowledge of Vienna marks him out as a Viennese musician through and through. And yet in every sentence he speaks and every phrase he utters he reveals that he is just as much at home in Berlin and that the Berlin Philharmonic is just as much his work as the Grosses Festspielhaus in Salzburg. A single town, even a single country are palpably too small for him, he always thinks in larger dimensions and sees his sphere of influence literally everywhere. His music films, for example, really are his message and legacy to the world; when he speaks of their impact and therefore also of their audience, the vista quickly opens up and he begins to talk about Japanese commercial practices and the standards that currently apply in the USA.

During the years of which he has been talking, a technical development has taken place which in part, at least, has been very much after his own heart. In his own view, today's interpreter no longer finds his audience in the opera house or concert hall, nor indeed through worldwide tours or through loyalty towards a small and manageable circle of grateful music lovers. Today's interpreter must come to terms with technology and convince a worldwide audience through the medium of technology.

How often during recent years has Herbert von Karajan been able to see for himself that even on tour he can appeal to only a small élite band of music lovers, whereas television broadcasts allow him to reach an audience that can be numbered in millions. And now that he has convinced himself that, in the field of technology, standards have been reached, or soon will be reached, which seem to him to be acceptable, he now concentrates his attention on an audience which can be numbered in millions, scattered as it is throughout the entire world.

Why should he present himself as an Austrian, as a Salzburger, or even as a Berliner, however great his attachment and loyalty towards individual towns and institutions? Whatever he has to say, one always has the impression that he is at pains to avoid all local associations. He belongs to the world which he assumes belongs to him. This is an attitude which even his colleagues and his orchestras cannot assume so readily. They are the Berlin Philharmonic or the Vienna Philharmonic, they belong in the Philharmonie or in the Musikverein – and they regard themselves, of course, as an essential part of the Berlin Festwochen or the Salzburg Festival.

But Herbert von Karajan, who once declared in this context that there would always be a festival wherever he appeared, refuses to be bound to a place either by decades of living there or by being given the freedom of the cities where he works. It doesn't suit his nature. It doesn't suit his plans, plans which he has already fixed in his mind once and for all.

As a result, tensions spring up, differences of opinion that are difficult to describe and which are never properly discussed. Anyone who works with Herbert von Karajan in Berlin, Salzburg or Vienna will find Berlin, Salzburg or Vienna the centre of his life at least for the present. For Karajan they are merely places which happen to coincide with his grand scheme of things either by chance or because of plans which have long since been laid. For Karajan, Karajan is the man who has arranged everything just as it is.

To the Vienna Opera

In addition to his positions in Berlin, Milan and Salzburg, Herbert von Karajan now received an invitation to take over the Vienna State Opera. It was 1956. Although he had recently conducted exemplary performances of operas in Vienna, they had all been concert performances in the Grosser Musikvereinssaal. Audiences and critics alike described these performances as an audible knocking at the doors of the State Opera, though even today Karajan himself refuses to accept that description. 'It wasn't meant like that. I saw how difficult it was to prepare performances that were ideally cast and adequately rehearsed, given what was going on in the opera business all over the world. And so I wanted to treat myself to the luxury of conducting the occasional concert performance of a work that would be of a standard that I myself desired. The Musikverein, together with the very many friends who were active there, seemed the obvious choice.' He was concerned to achieve what he himself describes as 'optimal quality', not to find a quick solution to the problem of the State Opera, a problem which he himself did not see as such.

When the director of the federal theatre administration, Ernst Marboe, invited Karajan to a first round of talks, the Vienna Opera had only just been reopened. Karl Böhm was its legitimate conductor and had just been acclaimed at the opening ceremony. Of course, Böhm was then on the threshold of an international career and, having worked exclusively in Vienna for months on end, was now undertaking his first conducting engagements abroad. There were opera fans who refused to accept that, and there were loyal supporters of Böhm who would not have appreciated 'secret negotiations' with Karajan. If one accepts

Karajan's version of events, he was not interested in taking over the Vienna Opera, and certainly not in taking it over under the circumstances then prevailing.

'My talks with Marboe made little progress. And I really wasn't sure whether I wanted to be artistic director in Vienna. I made my conditions clear from the outset and said that I didn't want to be simply director of the opera. Certainly, I had plenty of experience and knew how the organization was run. But I also knew how much work is involved in such a job. And I stressed in particular that I didn't want to take on this work because I knew it too well. But then there were talks with the then Finance Minister, Reinhard Kamitz. He was an important man, it was he, so to speak, who was responsible for the economic miracle in Austria, and even today he is still highly regarded by politicians of all parties. When I went to see him, he told me that he knew all about the situation at the State Opera and that he had also looked into the house's financial problems. It had become clear to him in the light of my earlier discussions with Marboe that a house that was run according to my own ideas and demands would not be cheap. But he told me – and these were his actual words – that he would make everything available that the house needed. If I were not to take over as director, the money would certainly not be available to anyone else.'

This is a conversation which Herbert von Karajan has repeated countless times. And each time he gets to what must have been an irresistible offer, he quotes himself, saying, 'Minister, you have caught me' and he shows, always adopting the same gesture, how he held out his hands to the Finance Minister. There are few situations in Karajan's life which he retells so often and so consistently. Here is a relatively small country with an absolutely great opera house. Here is Karajan himself, requesting hitherto unheard-of sums of money for the artistic directorship of this house (a position which is said to be the life's dream of every other Viennese adult) and arriving, moreover, with plans which must have seemed revolutionary. And not only is it agreed that he can put his ideas into practice, he is told that he is the only man who can do so. No one else would have been given the same opportunity.

And Karajan continues to speak enthusiastically about the Minister. 'Kamitz kept his word. I had been in Vienna for scarcely three months when there was an increase in the level of taxation which had immediate repercussions for the State Opera's budget. When I telephoned the Finance Minister to explain the problem to him, he told me that he had known about it for some time and had already dealt with the problem. As indeed he had. Kamitz had known for a long time what was in the offing, and he'd taken precautionary measures. And that's how the situation remained as long as Kamitz was Finance Minister. The State Opera functioned perfectly, as far as our financial position was concerned. It gave me pleasure to be able to tell Kamitz recently that I should probably not have left the State Opera if he had still been Finance Minister. I mean, perhaps that's not the whole truth. But I still feel so indebted to him that it would have made my departure from Vienna more difficult.'

The many years that Karajan spent at the State Opera were a time of jubilation but also of carping criticism among Karajan watchers; but in the eyes of Vienna's opera lovers they were not just an era, they marked the beginning of a new epoch. Karajan forged close links with La Scala, Milan and was consistent in his approach to performances in the original language (an example which other opera houses soon followed). He took charge of a series of first nights, brought leading guest artists into the house – and he himself staged his own productions with passionate commitment.

And yet, like every other opera director in Vienna, he was drawn into the maelstrom of criticism and cultural politics and subjected to a workload which no single artist should be asked to bear. Decades later, at a time when all the problems of that period have become operatic history, he sums up his time in Vienna in terms far removed from the sensational interviews which he gave at the time of his demonstrative departure from the city.

'During my time at the State Opera I learned a vast amount of new things. Of course, it was important for me and for the house that I came to Vienna with a great deal of existing experience. Ever since my first appointment in Ulm I had made a point of learning how an opera house works and of having a say in its running. If you reckon all the years I spent in Ulm, Aachen and Berlin, I had a good thirty years' experience behind me when I came to the State Opera. And I know now that there's no other way. A house of that size and that standard can be run only by someone who has learned the business of being an opera director and who has been doing it for decades. Otherwise one should not risk taking on a job like the one in Vienna.' No one knows better than Karajan that even after he had left Vienna, there were still conductors who dared to take on the job with too little experience in this difficult area. If he refrains from criticizing his successors, it is because he knows that he is basically of the same mind as many members of the Vienna State Opera, he knows them, works with them in Salzburg and yet does not discuss with them his views on other conductors. If he speaks of another conductor, it is because he has something positive to say.

'What I really learned during my time at the State Opera was chiefly, as always, the tools of the trade. From the outset I became deeply involved in stage technology, I discovered how outstandingly good the technical crew are in Vienna, I was on an almost friendly footing with these people at all the rehearsals. On stage, with the lighting technicians, and in the workshops, I learned all that I still had to learn as a producer. Above all, however, I realized that a house of this size is simply unmanageable – you have to subordinate yourself to its running if you want to keep it in working order. It has certain rules which cannot be contravened with impunity.' Karajan does not of course mean that, as an artist, one cannot alter or achieve anything at the State Opera. But what he does mean, as he demonstrates even today at his rehearsals and performances in Salzburg, is that you have to secure the support of the entire set-up.

To give a single example (an example which he himself sets, even if he does not refer to it): when he is in Salzburg, rehearsing for his own productions, the colleagues who make themselves available to him are generally from the Vienna State Opera. And not only does he know them all by name, he even knows their preferences and peculiarities, preferences which he is prepared to acknowledge. He welcomes them and chats with them, and sometimes even asks them for their opinion: he takes this for granted, although he knows that things are not always like this in the major opera houses. I have been present when, during the most intensive rehearsal period, he has found time to discuss with his stage crew the appearance of a larger-than-life-size statue from *Aida* in the garden of the set designer Günther Schneider-Siemssen and to consider how astonished the latter will be at an ornament so out of keeping with its surroundings. I have been present when he showed concern for his stage manager after the latter had suffered a fainting fit during a rehearsal. And I have been present when he sensed trouble brewing on stage and settled the potential dispute with a few polite words relayed by loudspeaker from his rehearsal desk in the stalls.

Of course, his productions in Salzburg are now rehearsed under conditions which he himself has struggled hard to achieve and which he regards as ideal. And he prefers not to talk about the conditions under which he once had to work in Vienna. But when he does so, there is no trace of self-pity or regret in what he has to say. Only satisfaction that he achieved something in Vienna at the State Opera and that he learned something there.

'When I left Vienna, it was not at all clear to me what had gone wrong. I realize now that the conditions I demanded then could not be met in an opera house that operated a repertory system. You only have to remember what we achieved and where we almost failed completely: I engaged all the singers from the Milan opera. We heard the greatest, most beautiful voices in the world at the State Opera. And although these singers were certainly not cheap, the so-called house singers were much more expensive, and still are. They had, and still have, contracts for such and such a number of appearances which are neither demanded nor wanted of them. In other words, they are ultimately paid much more than they would get for their appearances if they were to be engaged only as guest artists.

'And there's something else I worked out for myself. Although you may begin by regarding it as ideal if every opera performance causes a sensation, what this means is that people start to make demands that simply cannot be met. There are not enough sensational singers in the world to perform, evening after evening, in even a single opera house and always maintain the highest standards. There may be only two outstanding tenors at any one time. You'd have difficulty finding even a third outstanding tenor.

'It is clear to me now that my long-cherished plan to amalgamate six major opera houses might have overcome some of the difficulties, but that it wouldn't have been realizable in the long term. What I thought at the time was that an ideal ensemble could be signed up for each of the important operas, they would sing the première at one house and then, after an appropriate interval and according to a precisely arranged plan, change to another house, under the conductor who was responsible for that particular production. In time something like a regular rota would have emerged, with all these ensembles going from house to house, allowing audiences everywhere to hear well prepared and, so to speak, ideal productions. I now know that not even the general public would have bought that; the audience would grow tired and feel sated in an opera house where, night after night, the same first-night quality was always on offer. Whatever else you may try, you'll not achieve any better results in an opera house than I achieved during my time in Vienna: with around 300 performances a season we had perhaps forty very good ones at which everyone on stage, in the orchestra and in the audience was satisfied. The rest were, so to speak, decent routine, certainly nothing to be ashamed about. And at least 100 performances every season were absolutely terrible, even during my own era. There was nothing that could be done at the time to change things, even today there's not an opera director alive who can improve the situation.'

I do not think Herbert von Karajan has ever spoken so openly before about the Karajan years in Vienna. Long after his departure from the city, he thought of returning there for special festive occasions, and for a number of years he was even persuaded to give a series of performances at the State Opera, although he did not realize his idea of having the company perform only under his control for a month each year. However fascinating it may have sounded, the idea was impracticable,

Herbert von Karajan conducting the Vienna Philharmonic in Vienna's Grosser Musikvereinssaal. (*Harry Weber*)

Karajan conducting the opening of the Philharmonic Ball in Vienna.
(*Franz Goess*)

Eliette and Herbert von Karajan at the Opera Ball. (*Franz Goess*)

With Jean Cocteau, who appeared for the maestro at the Vienna State Opera. (*Barbara Pflaum*)

Herbert von Karajan in Salzburg. (*Ferdinand Schreiber*)

With Rudolf Gamsjäger, visiting the Vienna Konzerthaus during rehearsals for a concert with Karlheinz Stockhausen, Pierre Boulez and Bruno Maderna. (*Elfriede Hanak*)

At the Vienna State Opera, Karajan introduces the last of his fellow directors, Egon Hilbert. (*Heinz Hosch*)

Herbert von Karajan with the general secretary of the Salzburg Festival, Tassilo Nekola, and the Festival president, Bernhard Paumgartner. (*Max Reinhardt Research Institute*)

With Rudolf Gamsjäger, for many years general secretary of the Gesellschaft der Musikfreunde, and later director of the Vienna State. (*Rudolf Blaha*)

After a concert at the Musikverein. (*Rudolf Blaha*)

With Henri Clouzot, with whom he had his first experience of producing music films. (*Fritz Kern*)

A curtain call after a performance of *The Valkyrie* at the 1968 Salzburg Easter Festival. With Régine Crespin, Gundula Janowitz and Thomas Stewart. (*Max Reinhardt Research Institute*)

Herbert von Karajan signing a contract in Salzburg with (l. to r.) the business mar
of the Philharmonic Herr Resel, the director of Telemondial Uli Märkle.
Philharmonic chairman Herr Altenburger and the Festival president Albert M
(*Gabriela Brandenstein*)

Herbert von Karajan with Pope John II on the occasion of a performance of (
Mozart's Masses in St Peter's. (*Arturo Mari*)

With José Carreras, rehearsing *Don Carlos* for the Salzburg Easter Festival. (*Siegfried Lauterwasser*)

Herbert von Karajan conducting his first New Year's Day concert in 1987. (*Erich Lessing*)

although it met with no resistance on the part of the artists, the director, or even the management. Only the fact that a major opera house simply cannot afford to offer a tenth month of festival performances after nine months of continuous work and, at the same time, expend energies that are also required on occasion during the other nine months reduced the planned 'Herbert von Karajan Festival' to a handful of sensational guest performances, some of which were subject to the additional stresses of being broadcast on television. Karajan withdrew from the project when he realized that he was wearing himself out.

'During my time at the State Opera I was also party to a number of so-called "necessary compromises", which I learned to hate. It's all so long ago and I've almost forgotten about it, though other people still remember. I recall preparing one particular new production in the house. We worked on it all day and when, at the end of the rehearsal, I was about to go into the director's box to look in briefly on the performance, the box attendant said to me, "That was lucky. The conductor only just made it in time from Buenos Aires. He got into Vienna at five o'clock this afternoon." And I thought that here was another performance for which I was responsible, where a great deal would no doubt have to be left to improvisation.

'And another example: I remember once telling the long-standing head of opera planning Ernst August Schneider in no uncertain terms that a particular soprano should not be allowed to keep on singing this or that part. I then went abroad, thinking that at least one minor matter had been settled. When I got back to Vienna, I saw the poster for the evening's performance, and there on the cast list was the name of the soprano: she was down for the very part I didn't want to hear her singing at the State Opera. Of course, I immediately telephoned Ernst August Schneider. And his answer to my reproach? "You were right, Herr von Karajan. But, look, it was her birthday, and she so wanted to be allowed to sing . . ." It was a touching little story, typically Viennese. But it was the sort of thing that went on at the Vienna State Opera more than once, and there was nothing even I could do where such trivialities were concerned.

'I learned how to develop a feeling for one's house. I remember visiting the workshops. The head carpenter fascinated me. He always knew exactly how much wood and how many nails were still in stock. He told me that he sensed instinctively whenever anything had been stolen from his workshop. It reminds me of Princess Thurn und Taxis, who was a member of the same family that gave such great encouragement to Rainer Maria Rilke. She told me once that a real housewife can sense when something is being stolen from her household. "You can smell when treachery's afoot," she said. I know now what the head of the state theatres' carpentry workshop and the Princess were trying to tell me: as boss of a major opera house, you need to be able to sense whether everything is in order in the house, you need to have an idea of when is the right time to intervene. That is something else I learned at the State Opera.

'Of course, there were rows and major incidents which never failed to cause a public stir. But I know now that I would not have left the State Opera because of these disagreements, which always took place at the highest level and on the front pages of the daily newspapers. It was the little things that got on top of me, the daily annoyances, I grew tired of the system. I still remember our attempt to get Egon Hilbert on to the board of directors. I gave him two weeks of my time, we went on walks together and I explained to him what my ideas were for the State Opera. He then came to the house and from the very first moment tried to do the exact opposite. He spoke of a modified ensemble theatre. I said there was no such thing. But he refused to accept what I said. We very soon found ourselves holding diametrically opposed ideas.

'I sensed this. Basically I'd already decided to go to Salzburg and, soon after that, to found my own festival. However much I'd learned during my time in Vienna, I was ultimately unhappy. I had to get away.'

No one will ever forget the arguments that took place, involving not only ministers but the Federal Chancellor himself, but Herbert von Karajan had nothing more to say about those last hectic days in Vienna, about the interviews he gave at the time, and about the efforts, ultimately crowned by success, of the Salzburg Festival board of directors to keep him in Austria at least for the summer months. I am happy to put it on record that, as a witness to the events in question, I should have been only too pleased to have been able to document Karajan's own comments, not least for the benefit of Vienna's opera fans. But the conductor could not be persuaded to say any more on the subject.

During his years at the Vienna State Opera Herbert von Karajan conducted thirty different operas, in other words, virtually the whole of the repertory that he himself describes as necessary and valid today. However, there were a number of Mozart operas which he did not conduct, he did not tackle Richard Strauss, and he did not himself produce the whole of Verdi. By way of compensation he championed Monteverdi, Ildebrando Pizzetti and Igor Stravinsky and at least for some of their performances insisted on conducting them himself. Almost half of the operas he conducted were also produced by him. His admirers scarcely need to be reminded of the public debates which he fired, often while rehearsals were still in progress, and of the most violent reactions which his productions provoked. They still remember these reactions, or, if their memories have grown indistinct, that is no bad thing. Karajan's comments on his time in Vienna are not conducted in passionate terms.

The same is true of Karajan's colleagues from what now seems to him a remote period of his past. He remembers them and generally speaks of them with great warmth. But to recall them in the context of his own past is something he finds deeply uninteresting. Even in reply to his interviewer's insistent questioning as to whether he would not like to have some of the singers available now who were acclaimed with him then and make recordings with them, he reacts in an unsentimental way. Time has not stood still, is the gist of his reply. Some of the singers with whom he collaborated to produce many of the greatest evenings in the opera house have no real successors. They do not exist, and so there is no point in talking about them. If he thinks about the question, or if he plunges into the effortful routine of auditioning singers, as he so often does, what he is looking for are singers who are available now, singers with whom he can perform today and in the future. He then asks himself how he can interpret Mozart convincingly with today's artists. And he plans more intensively for 1991 than for a commemorative chapter dealing with the period between 1945 and 1987. Karajan has little time in his memoirs for those typical opera lovers who are almost more interested in the past than they are in the present. He is wholeheartedly committed to the present and to the future.

Indeed, he is so concerned for the future that he keeps on devising courses or measures to build up a new Mozart ensemble out of the vocal material that is available to him now. It is not a selfless undertaking, but one which he assumes in his capacity as a member of the Salzburg Festival committee, since he recognizes that very many Mozart singers will soon have their chance to sing, but that very few will offer themselves of their own accord. Karajan has already organized several internal competitions and frequently invited experienced interpreters like Peter Schreier to assume responsibility for completing the training of these young singers. Sometimes he has used journalists for this purpose and launched a kind of campaign, but has then finished up achieving his goal diplomatically and silently. 'There's no doubt one should look to the next generation of singers. I am always hearing young singers, and each time I think that many of them still need working with intensively before they are let loose on the circuit, which destroys them far too quickly. It's the same with singers as it is with young conductors: nowhere are there opera houses or directors who feel fully responsible for young artists and who plan for them over the years. And there are of course far too few young artists who are themselves sensible enough to choose a slow, natural career for themselves. They all allow themselves to be led astray by seductive offers, so that their voices are very soon ruined, or else they never even reach the point of beginning to develop properly.'

Karajan does not join in the chorus of those who claim that there is less quality among young musicians now than there was in the good old days. He is always finding enough fresh material, and he is always prepared to praise his current singers to the skies. In order to present them properly, he even takes on commitments which he had not otherwise anticipated in his long-standing plans. For example, he made a recording with

Anna Tomowa-Sintow in which the soprano sang the closing scene from *Capriccio* under Karajan's baton.

Karajan of course says little about all this, preferring to give only the vaguest hints in his autobiography. What is involved here, after all, are the strains and stresses which any conductor and committee member has to put up with as a matter of course.

And if there is a trace of inconsistency about Karajan's attitude here as elsewhere, it is to be found only in the area of personal involvement. Karajan, who left the Vienna State Opera decades ago because he was tired of detailed work and having to worry about organizational problems, is now devoting his time to precisely that. In areas where one would scarcely expect to find him active, he worries about the Festival's casting problems and has an eye for errors in drawing up contracts, errors which no one else has noticed but which seem to him important. His colleagues, who have some idea of this additional burden, are either enjoined to silence or inured to it. And if ever they are tempted to be indiscreet, they know only too well that it would not do to find what they have said reproduced in a book.

Anyone interviewing Herbert von Karajan finds it difficult to elicit information about his fellow directors in Vienna. They were honourable men who have either remained extremely loyal to him (one thinks, for example, of the President of the Salzburg Festival, Albert Moser), or who are long since dead and therefore not a subject for discussion – men like the producer Oscar Fritz Schuh, who it was hoped would save the situation in Vienna, but who was reluctant to come to the city, the enthusiastic Egon Hilbert, who wanted to enter into a strange alliance with Karajan but who could then not bring himself to agree to all of Karajan's plans, the Stuttgart intendant Walter Erich Schäfer, who spent two years in Vienna without ever settling in the city, and the opera lover Egon Seefehlner, who later became director in Vienna and who, on taking up his office, had the brief pleasure of being able to announce a reconciliation between Karajan and the Vienna Opera. They all no doubt played a role during Herbert von Karajan's days in Vienna. But they all become curiously shadowy whenever one talks to Karajan about his former times in the city, wherever he may be in the world at the time. The eighty-year-old conductor prefers to recall minor personal incidents, such as the story of a flute player in the Vienna Philharmonic, rather than discuss major complaints or insights concerning his former fellow directors.

The reason is not hard to find. Time and again Karajan freely admits that he has little time for discussions or arguments about his own opinions or wishes. Time and again he declares his support for the system which he devised for himself in Salzburg following his departure from Vienna. Time and again he suppresses all memory of people with whom he has had to discuss administrative or even artistic questions. He has probably never liked doing so. No doubt he would like to have had undisputed control over a large house in Vienna, a house which, for all its problems, ought to have submitted to his will without difficulty. But when he finally saw that that was impossible, he came to the obvious conclusion, conducted at the Salzburg Festival, and, literally during one of the shortest imaginable intervals, conceived the idea of the Salzburg Easter Festival. His own festival.

Memories of his youth and student years bound him to the Salzburg Festival, the close links of the difficult post-war years when everyone regarded him as the secret promoter of the first performances in 1946 and 1947. But what bound him most of all to the Salzburg Festival was his sympathy for a system which gave him the best guarantee possible that the working conditions he desired could be realized there and which allowed those of his colleagues who had suffered under pressure of time and the repertory system in Vienna to work under favourable conditions during the summer months. When Karajan decided to sit on the board of directors in Salzburg and remain available as producer and conductor, his decision meant that he would continue working with singers from the State Opera, with the State Opera Chorus and with the members of the State Opera Orchestra who functioned under their more brilliant title of 'Vienna Philharmonic'. In other words, he could prepare and perform State Opera performances without exposing himself to the danger of having to put up with State Opera routine.

94

The Easter Festival

'People have talked a great deal about the origins of the Easter Festival. What started it all off was a remark by the conductor Christoph von Dohnányi, who told me I should produce operas with myself in sole charge and according to my own standards. It gave me food for thought and at the same time reminded me of what was then my unfulfilled dream of producing Wagner's operas again, this time under ideal conditions. The plan for the Easter Festival was conceived fairly quickly, the necessary budget was worked out with Michel Glotz on a flight to Stockholm, where I was going to audition singers. I may add that, much later, when the first Festival came about, the budget proved to be spot on. We first thought of carrying out the project in Geneva but weren't sure what to do about the orchestra. But then, as I've often described in the past, there was an evening at the Salzburg Festival. I was conducting *Boris Godunov*, and was standing on the podium during the short break before the great choral scene, and suddenly I knew that I should hold the Easter Festival in this house with these artists. You've already got everything you need here, I thought. I drove home after the performance, went out into the pouring rain and walked around the surrounding area here for two hours, by which time the whole plan for an Easter Festival was firmly fixed in my head.'

Many of the interviews which Herbert von Karajan has given contain this same highly detailed account. It is, of course, understandable that after so many years the conductor should always recall the birth of his own Festival in this way rather than any other. After all, that was how he originally felt it to be and that is how he has always retold the story in such immensely effective detail; a version of events has taken root in his memory which will be retold in this way and no other until the end of his days. Whether he had already begun to think of the Grosses Festspielhaus in Salzburg long before the brief interval during *Boris Godunov* and whether he actually foresaw and solved all the associated problems that same evening in the course of a single walk is beside the point. He has fixed the moment of birth of his Festival for all time, and that's how it will remain. Even if it were possible to demonstrate by means of documents, letters or the reminiscences of contemporary witnesses that the version needed correcting, there would be no point in doing so as far as he himself is concerned. Why should he correct his own memories?

'We reckoned at that time that we'd get by without a subsidy for the rehearsals which would already have had to have taken place for the recording we intended to make in advance, and for the corresponding contracts with all the participants. And we did indeed survive the first Easter Festival – there was even a tiny surplus. And I renounced any fee – that goes without saying.' As his present interviewer well recalls, never before or since has Karajan been so visibly happy and in such a good mood as he was immediately before the first performances at his Easter Festival in Salzburg. He acted as a charming host to the journalists from outside, he was to be seen in the town, chattering with people he normally scarcely noticed. He had realized his life's dream, you could tell just by looking at him.

'It was of course only to be foreseen that things would change very quickly. Everyone realized how much they could earn at the Easter Festival, too. All the prices immediately shot up. And all the expenses went up at a tremendous rate. And so it was entirely right and logical that we received compensation in the event of cancellation, since the Festival brought new advantages not only for the artists but also for the whole town.' Although Karajan had not been committed to this idea for very long, events have proved him right, not least in view of the fact that Salzburg's two major Festivals have finally found a means of peaceful coexistence. No one would now contest his right to regard the public subsidy as a necessary tribute inasmuch as all of his Salzburg productions attract cosmopolitan audiences to the town. His Easter Festival is credited with the same advantages as the Salzburg Festival itself: not only does it stimulate the local economy, its support for that economy is out of all proportion to any disadvantages involved, while, at the same time, it has turned what used to be described as the 'dead season' into the second most popular tourist season of the year.

'I believe we've achieved everything with the Easter Festival that I set out to do. There have been performances which I have been able to prepare over a period of two years, just as I once dreamed of doing. And we have only ever taken up operas into the repertory when I was certain that I had the ideal cast at my disposal.'

The conversations which make up this biography of Herbert von Karajan began during rehearsals and breaks in rehearsals for the Easter Festival production of *Lohengrin*. Karajan seemed never to tire. He always had a few words of keen encouragement for the extras whose task it was to substitute for the soloists by standing still on stage during lighting rehearsals and who themselves were far too quick to tire. And he commented in highly militaristic fashion on the processions and groupings that were enacted on stage with less than military precision. What he muttered in between times might have marked him out as an old soldier, but it was only despair at the fact that people on stage are far less easy to discipline than musicians ever are. He had first used members of the Austrian armed forces in crowd scenes while still at the State Opera, and he still uses them here in Salzburg. But he manages to avoid the impression that the soldiers in question have been drilled to march in step across the Salzburg stage or that they are especially suited to holding their lances at approximately the same angle of inclination. His concern for detail is something he has no difficulty in explaining. He never receives credit or criticism if his Elsa makes a correct or incorrect gesture, whereas he is always held to account for the peripheral details, which in a Wagner opera are the ones that tend to get noticed. They also irritate him as a conductor if they are imprecise, just as he always used to be irritated by the production moves and stage pictures of designers who did not work according to his own instructions.

'I gladly admit that the fact that I can produce exclusively

97

according to my own ideas leaves its mark on the musical interpretation, too. I can give you an example. As long as I had to conduct the transformation music in *Parsifal* as an accompaniment to completely impossible events on stage, I chose much faster speeds than I should have done. I now realize that my only reason for rushing this glorious music was to escape from these images. Now that I have my own production, these tempi have become calm and relaxed and I think they are now finally correct. Because I'm not distracted or irritated by what's going on on stage.'

Wherever possible, a sympathetic lighting plan is worked out for musical sequences. An assistant sits by the tape recorder and at least two lighting technicians make a note in their scores of the exact number of bars during which one lighting cue will change and fade into another. Karajan himself not only knows the exact number of bars involved, he also knows precisely what mood he wants to create. In *Lohengrin*, for example, he was looking for a blue which did not exist in nature but which he recommended to his lighting technicians as the blue which one sees when an ophthalmologist trains his torch on one's eye in order to examine it. A close approximation of this blue was obtained on the Festspielhaus stage, and Karajan at least was of the opinion that the performers should allow their actions to be influenced by this kind of blue. In demanding this, he required his singers to do the exact opposite of what, according to his own accounts, unmusical producers all too often demand: where they demand more and more movement, Karajan insists on an extreme reduction in the number and type of gestures and moves. 'Clever singers understand that. Calm and concentration on the music can be achieved by leaving out everything unnecessary. And what can be more important in an opera than to concentrate on the music?' It is still difficult to contradict Karajan.

It doesn't worry him that internationally acclaimed singers occasionally leave him in the lurch during his Easter Festival productions – and especially during *Lohengrin*. He is even less worried now that he has seen some more recent productions which so scandalize present-day audiences. Herbert von Karajan knows all about the so-called 'new' Mozart style, he has seen some recent Bayreuth productions, even if only in part, and he is familiar with a great many other productions which he has seen on television and which he sometimes talks about. He sums up his concept of opera production, a concept valid for his entire period in Salzburg, though more especially of course for his Easter Festival, in a single sentence, 'With me there is no falsifying of documents.' In conversation he applies this notion to the music, explaining that orchestral players tend not to hold on to notes for their full value. But when it is productions which are at issue, he describes almost all the actions which producers think up in order to liven up the stage or to give a scene a 'symbolic character' as 'falsifying the documents'.

With his departure from Vienna, his concentration on Salzburg and the institutionalization of the Easter Festival Herbert von Karajan has embarked on a new phase of artistic endeavour, a phase he would now describe as probably his last and most productive period if there were not a decisive break in his life at this point. His serious illnesses, his operations and his increasing infirmity all came at a time when he needed his strength more than ever.

'Perhaps people have never really noticed, but it is a long time now since I began to concentrate my work on only two orchestras and only two institutions. I gave up almost all guest appearances far longer ago than people think, and if I've prepared operas in Berlin or given concerts, it has been only with the Berlin and Vienna Philharmonics.' With few exceptions, this is indeed the case: Karajan has kept his word and created fixed points to which he has devoted all his energies while knowing how to use those energies to maximum effect. Although it has often come in for abuse, his method of deploying those media which have been perfected in recent years, using concerts for recordings and music films, and staging opera productions in conjunction with gramophone recordings and television broadcasts is partly a way of making up for endless world tours and partly an attempt to give fixed form to what he is doing.

Always inspired by new technology, Herbert von Karajan is a man whose name is inextricably linked with fast cars, in other words, with cars that are technically highly sophisticated. As the

99

owner of an unbeaten racing yacht and the pilot of an equally sophisticated private jet he has kept abreast of technology here, too, while ensuring that he remains an object of general envy. In conversation he tells in great detail of his involvement in the medium of gramophone recordings from its beginnings to the age of the compact disc. And he is still of the opinion that he was right to express his clear initial objections to the medium of television. He can supply ample evidence for both of these claims. Evidence which, in the form of many historic and an infinite number of more recent recordings, supports his close links with the medium of records, but which also justifies his original doubts about the video recordings of concerts which he recorded with the Berlin Philharmonic and which he now shows in his own studios as though they were a caricature of the real thing. In addition, there are his successful attempts to persuade television channels to increase the sound quality of their transmissions.

These are topics on which Herbert von Karajan does not need to be asked his opinion. Interviewers who have the good fortune to be allowed to speak to the maestro can tell a thing or two about the speed with which he has an answer to virtually every question about his work in the recording studio and about the rapid technological progress that has taken place in recent years. I may claim for myself that at almost every session which was intended to take us back into Karajan's past, I found myself confronted by his total fixation on the subject of records and films.

That technical and artistic questions become indistinguishable here is self-evident with Herbert von Karajan. That his marginal comments on technological progress and the artist's need to come to terms with technology allow one to deduce his views on almost every other topic, too, perhaps makes it easier in this second, major part of his autobiography to present a fraction of what Karajan himself sees as his most important work in his eightieth year.

His colleagues grow politely desperate when, at Karajan's express request, they have to work with him at rehearsals and recordings, at final sessions and playbacks, in the cutting room and at meetings to discuss individual sequences in a music film.

They have to give him their full concentration, and they probably think he is barely distracted by passing visitors whom, patient and enthusiastic as always, he introduces to his great work. What they overlook is that Herbert von Karajan may sometimes need this distraction. He has built up his own world, a world he could continue to work on for decades to come, and he has to explain this new world of his both to himself and to others. Otherwise it might be misunderstood.

Summarized as briefly as possible in a form which Karajan himself would certainly not adopt, what is involved here is an attempt to preserve his principal repertory not only on records and compact discs but also visually on film. And to do so with great consistency in a form which, perfected on the basis of many experiments, he now declares to be suited to his purpose. It distresses him deeply, however, that the technological progress to which he so often appeals is still far from achieving an ideal solution, especially in the area of visual recording. It seems more or less certain that the sound quality will not be radically revolutionized in the foreseeable future, but it is totally uncertain which of the present possibilities of recording the visual image will prove the most durable and, at the same time, the most popular. Opinions have already changed again recently, and it will be some time before it is clear how durable all the different materials are that are currently being tested.

Herbert von Karajan's oft-repeated remark that he would like to be at least ten years younger has nothing to do with the fact that he would like to blot out the last ten years of his life, years which have brought him a great deal of pain. It relates, rather, to the fact that he would like to make and produce his music films in the present, but using methods that will not become available until some time in the future. His aim is to leave behind him films which not only reflect his aims and intentions but which are in keeping with the demands that he makes of material and technology.

Karajan has talked about the topic we were supposed to be discussing, but at the same time, as always, it is a form of visual instruction that he has offered. He has explained what he wants and also, of course, why he wants it.

'Concerts were filmed even during Toscanini's and Furt-wängler's day. Of course, at that time they didn't have today's means or the interest in music films which we can take for granted nowadays. So what do we see when these historic recordings are shown to us now? Filmed concerts, in which we see the conductor from the side or from the back, and an orchestra which as good as never appears, except as an anonymous mass. Never for a moment do we see what interests us most of all, the link between the music, the conductor and the orchestra.'

Anyone who has had the good fortune on even one occasion in his life to slip into an orchestra rehearsal knows immediately what Karajan means. The few archival films that exist of Wilhelm Furtwängler or the very old Arturo Toscanini give the music lover scarcely more than a hint of how these musicians conducted. Quite apart from the technical quality, they give us far less of the personality of these historic figures than, say, an old shellac recording gives us of the timbre of Enrico Caruso's voice. Toscanini and Furtwängler seem more real to us in the simple accounts of older orchestral players than they do in these films.

'My first films were made in Vienna in collaboration with a first-rate film producer by the name of Henri Clouzot. They were films we made with the Vienna Symphonic in a studio and they required a tremendous amount of time, with the result that they were correspondingly expensive. For Clouzot came to us from the cinema and thought in terms of camera angles. That meant that we kept on having to change the set and perform in front of the camera, so that we worked for at least thirty-six hours on a single symphony until there was finally enough material to be worked on and sifted through before they could make a start on editing the film. None the less, Clouzot was an artist, he had tremendous sensitivity and gave me the chance to learn a great deal from him. He was an eminently musical person and therefore an exception among other possible producers – what he wanted to show was the individual performer, the orchestral player, with the orchestra as a group of many such individual musicians, all working together as artists. Even today I am still grateful to him for his interest and for the advice which he gave me at the time we were making those recordings.'

The recording sessions on the Rosenhügel in Vienna were an especial torment for the musicians, I remember. They had to wait patiently for Clouzot to devise some particular camera angle and then had to keep miming their parts to a perfect tape that had already been made of the piece. At that time neither singers nor players were as experienced in the medium of films as they are nowadays, and were scarcely able to bring the same interpretative intensity to their parts when the cameras were rolling as they were able to produce as a matter of course at any given moment during a genuine concert, when the music was being played for real. It surprises no one that at the time this work proved to be so tremendously difficult and financially irresponsible. Even considering what was then the equally low standard of televised concerts, this was not the course that a musician like Herbert von Karajan was prepared to take.

'Then came the period of creative producers. I myself lived through this period and I recall with horror what was seen on the screen at this time. The music was accompanied by images thought up by visual artists. Basically it was always either steel mills, volcanoes or the most varied natural moods that were shown. There was no serious contact with the music, you certainly couldn't speak of the visual interpretation of a work – that's something that had been done in Walt Disney's *Fantasia* in 1937 but never again since then. But we all made these films, some of them are still on the market, some of them have recently come on to the market as video discs in Japan and the USA, and it distresses me deeply not to be able to prevent it. But I no longer own the rights to these films, and so I can't have them banned, however much I detest them. They're simply hideous, and my only hope is that the video discs on which they are produced will prove to be a fairly cheap and not very durable commodity.

'Of course, there were soon films on which the orchestra could also be seen. I remember the absurd ideas that were conceived and realized at that time, what, for the players, were extremely comic positions for the orchestra to be placed in and the insane tracking shots which producers thought up, filming us from

above, and generally while we were performing Beethoven.'
Not only does Herbert von Karajan remember these films, he
also has copies of them and is only too pleased to show them
to his visitors. Curious though this situation is, it is one which I
myself have savoured. Karajan showed a music film conducted
by himself, expecting his visitor not merely to shake his head in
discreet disbelief but to laugh out loud at visual images which
he himself must once have accepted but which he now finds
risible at best. He evidently uses these examples of his own
films in order to remind himself how not to proceed in future.
He is mercilessly self-critical. Where one would assume that he
would at least put up with his *own* films from this period, he
is all too ready to make fun of himself.

'I believe that no musician has shown such intense interest in
this topic as I have. And now that my state of health very often
forces me to sit in front of a television screen, there is certainly
no one with such a comprehensive view of what's on offer. I
know of no other musician of standing who has taken such an
interest in music films and all their implications as I have. And
this in turn led me to take the next logical step, a long, long
time ago, when I was still producing operas myself. I realized
that the only way I could produce films according to my own
ideas was if I had wonderful colleagues and if I myself acted
as director. Only if I'm my own director does a film ultimately
express what I wanted to show.' Such words can be interpreted
and even turned against Karajan. But there is no trace of vanity
about them, they are spoken in all seriousness and mean nothing
more nor less than they say. Herbert von Karajan was dissatisfied
with certain visual interpreters, however sympathetic they may
otherwise have been; he never saw what he wanted to see on the
screen, and so one day, with a great deal of help from others, he
took over responsibility for directing his own films.

His colleagues have been constant and loyal to him for decades,
and he gives them all the credit that is due to them. He knows
very well that his cameraman needs few hints to tell what he
wants to see, and he knows that this, too, is a special skill. He
is full of enthusiasm for the sensitivity and musicality of his
young female cutter who can create dissolves lasting no more

than a fraction of a second, and who can do so, moreover, with sovereign mastery using a complicated digital system. He is happy to introduce the people he calls his 'team', which he does without condescension, impressing on outsiders that they are very important and highly competent and that they enjoy a high degree of personal responsibility. He admits, completely ungrudgingly, to those occasions when his assistants become his fellow workers and are capable of realizing his ideas even before they have been properly formulated. And he is full of praise for the teams that work for a private firm, available to assist him day and night when the need arises. He pays lavish tribute to a personal commitment that is unchecked by any trade union, and repeatedly emphasizes that it requires private initiative to achieve his particular kind of life's work.

'Technologically and financially it is, of course, very much easier now than it was two decades ago to realize my ideas. In principle it is all very straightforward. Before the actual recording takes place, we hire a youth orchestra which performs to an old tape recording under one of my assistants. This may not always be very satisfying for these young musicians, but it gives me the chance to work out all the camera angles long before the recording sessions take place and to solve as many of the lighting problems as possible before the orchestra assembles.

'What this means is that even before the orchestra players have arrived in the hall – even before we have begun to shoot the film – I can sort out many minor problems and make a number of corrections. This is less taxing on our nerves, it saves money, and it ensures a greater degree of peace and concentration during the recording sessions themselves.'

It is certainly true that the lighting rehearsals are tiring and unsatisfying for both the youth orchestra and for whichever conductor is in charge at the time. But it has to be musicians on the platform, in front of the cameras, since at this stage Karajan wants to be able to see things that he will not be able to check on later when he is conducting the recording. 'It appears to be minor details that are involved here. But these minor details are crucial and have to be right. I want to check, frame by frame, what will later be seen on screen. I want to be entirely certain that the violins are sitting in such a way that not a single bow bobs about in front of my nose later on. And I want to have the chance to discover at these rehearsals what a single violin bow may be capable of expressing. If you can establish the right moment for it to flicker like an oscillograph across the bottom of the screen, then the preliminary work will not only have achieved financial savings, it will also have provided you with an artistic gain.'

Herbert von Karajan aims for perfection by seeking to discover in advance where possible problems may arise and by eliminating them at source. He makes it possible, too, for the players to concentrate on the actual recordings by worrying them as little as is humanly feasible with technical problems. When he performs with them, he aims to solve those problems which could not be solved in advance, but by now the cameramen should know what is expected of them, and the lighting should already be finished. Sometimes it even is.

'And then the orchestra arrives, and we do two, at the most three, recordings. And the good thing about it is that the whole recording is now complete, and, what's more, live.'

Karajan long since grew disillusioned with dubbed recordings and now insists on recording live in the concert hall. He has developed a 'system' which he considers ideal and which he sticks to with great consistency. He begins by having all the cameras at his disposal positioned to the left of the orchestra, then for the second take he moves them all to the right. He has an additional camera in the orchestra permanently trained on the conductor, and later, when the work in question is played at a concert before an audience, he has another camera to film the result *in toto*, in order to have available the highly conventional image of the whole orchestra on the platform. By the end of the sessions, which sometimes take place over a period of two days, he has at least twelve, but often as many as sixteen, takes of a major symphony to serve as his raw material. The main advantage, as he himself points out, is that none of these reels comprises more than two takes, in other words, he has not mimed a concert to studio recordings but effectively has between twelve and sixteen live recordings which he can add to the films in his archives that still await editing.

106

These are the technical requirements, so to speak, that he is happy to discuss. More important to him, of course, are the artistic requirements, about which he has had little to say in public until now.

'After I'd made a number of recordings with film directors and television producers and had decided to be my own director, I shut myself away for two days in Italy with an expert. He helped me to find my way by asking me endless questions and offering a tremendous challenge. I'll never forget what he achieved with so seemingly simple a question as "What do you see?", nor what he was trying to provoke with his second question, which he kept on repeating, "What else can you see?"

'Let me give you a simple example. Two people come up to us. What can we see? Two people. A man and a woman? Two girls? Two men? What is so striking about them? How can we describe them more accurately? How are they walking? Are they walking side by side or are they walking with each other? But most of all, why are we interested in the fact that two people are coming towards us? What is it about them that seems so important that we notice it? What do we want to convey by means of this image of two people coming towards us?

'For two days I struggled to answer these apparently simple questions. I then realized what my questioner was trying to get at and what conclusions I should draw. He had shown me a problem in a filmic medium which I had known about for years and which I had had to solve every day of my life for decades. The problem was simply one of interpretation.'

For the next few paragraphs Herbert von Karajan will be allowed to speak uninterruptedly. For even in a transcript which, made up as it is of several different interviews, is not altogether authentic, his remarks on a subject that so preoccupies him need to be emphasized. The subject is interpretation.

'It's an age-old question, but what does the conductor actually do? What is he needed for? Isn't it enough for him to give the entries and do what he can to make sure that the musicians play the notes as exactly as possible as they appear in the score? Is there any further need for him?

'The answer to this question is complex. For basically there is scarcely a musician in the orchestra who is capable of describing even a single note in his part with the same degree of clarity as was demanded in the earlier example of the two people coming towards us. Because for each individual note which a composer has written there are very many questions and therefore very many answers that have to be found.

'For these questions never relate to the individual note alone, they involve not just its exact value, they can only be answered by someone who knows the whole context in which the note appears – both the individual part and all the parts that are being played at the same time. And even when these questions have all been answered, the conductor is still far from having identified all the problems and found solutions to them, he also has to take account of, and think about, the individual players and their relation to each other, not to mention the space in which they are performing and various other factors.

'And when you've reached that point, you have to remember, as a conductor, that composers of all ages have complained that they had only the most imperfect means of writing down their ideas – notes on a white sheet of paper between such and such a number of lines with a few accidentals and a few additional, generally accepted formulas, which, however, every composer thinks of in slightly different ways . . .

'Since this means that even a wholly exact rendition of all the composer's surviving instructions will probably not reproduce all the composer's ideas, I believe that a work of music does not start to exist the moment it is written down, nor even when what has been written down is played as exactly as possible. It begins to exist only when a conductor stands in front of an orchestra and conducts the piece on the basis of his understanding and his ideas. It is then that it starts to exist, coming to life in a new and different way each time it's performed, for it is very much a creative act which the conductor performs – and he, too, offers an interpretation that differs in nuance each time he conducts the work.

'Max Planck once said in a similar context that whenever you want to analyse a phenomenon, it changes at the very moment of analysis. As the simplest illustration of this claim I always take the example of a snowflake: as soon as you try to look at it more closely, it changes. On your hand, under the microscope . . .

'And what is true of every single white snowflake is also true of every single black dot, every note on the page. It changes as soon as you try to interpret it. But you have to interpret it, otherwise it is totally meaningless.

'That, in as few words as possible, is the most important challenge that a conductor has to face, leaving aside all the other problems that only arise during the rehearsal itself. That's interpretation.'

It is Karajan's express aim to give visual expression to this kind of interpretation with his music films too. He hopes to achieve that aim by having at his disposal as many takes as possible of every moment in a performance and by considering, bar by bar, how to express, by visual means, the musical relationships between them. It goes without saying, of course, that there will be no room here for shots of blast furnaces, erupting volcanoes or hazardous tracking shots above the heads of a full-size symphony orchestra. Such shots would distract the viewer and say nothing about the music as Karajan allows it to unfold.

The music film is therefore an ideal way for Karajan to convey his thoughts, since it allows him to force the listener to see exactly what he, Karajan, thinks a suitable means of representing the music.

In the concert hall the listener is more or less left to his own devices, he can watch the orchestra in its totality or follow the conductor giving exaggerated entries, but he will always be 'too late' and in many cases will fail to see in time which of the players on the platform has the 'most important' line at any given moment. In the concert hall, moreover, the listener is easily distracted and may lose himself for minutes on end in a detail of the ceiling architecture, or simply feel disturbed by another member of the audience.

Karajan argues that he is generally not offered what he really expects when he attends a concert, namely, the most effective possible introduction to the music. 'I can prove what I'm saying. When the Berlin Philharmonie was built and we moved into the new building, the subscribers were asked which seats they preferred. The first seats to be sold out, of course, were ones that had rarely been available in concert halls previously. Seats from which you had a direct view of the orchestra and the conductor. In the new house, which we conquered, so to speak, after a few preliminary experiments, and which we have learned to exploit in such a way that our playing now produces ideal acoustic conditions for every concertgoer, the seats which are always snapped up first are the ones where the audience is also close to the orchestra and can see the conductor's face.'

Like all other conductors, Karajan has to bear the reproach of laying emphasis upon superficialities and, as it were, stage-managing both his appearance and his gestures, but he sweeps aside all such considerations by explaining his attitude in detail.

On the one hand, it is self-evident to him that he must be visible to every member of the orchestra, even if, in accordance with tradition, they rarely look up from their music. On the other hand, he knows that each of his gestures serves not only to communicate with his players but also as a challenge to the audience. 'In a music film you can finally show the conductor properly. In doing so, you not only fulfil a wish on the part of the audience but you also help their understanding of the music, as long, that is, as the images are correctly deployed. There are so many moments in the course of a music film in which you also need to show the relationship between the conductor and the players in order to throw light on the score. And there are so many different moments in a music film in which you can offer help. For example, it's not only old-fashioned, it's positively wrong to concentrate only on the player who happens to be playing the most important line at any one time – sometimes you have to do so, sometimes you have to show only his instrument in order to symbolize the phrase, but there are other times when you have virtually to ignore the instrument and show only the intensity which the player himself brings to that moment. We have put all this to the test and come up with the most contradictory, mutually exclusive rules. A single violin bow, filmed at the right moment, can be made to represent the concentrated energy of an entire orchestra. Then, again, there are players who are shown drawing breath and who thus signal

110

something to us. But there is one thing that remains important throughout, namely, the need to find the right rhythm for every sequence of images, and to rid oneself of the belief that the music can be represented in a linear way.'

On the way back to his hotel from a series of retakes for one of his music films, Karajan demonstrates, without actually intending to, how important this feeling for rhythm is in every situation. He is being driven through Vienna during the worst part of the rush hour, and he repeatedly tells his driver the exact moment at which to start braking. If you breathe along with him, you feel, for the first time, that Karajan is capable of converting every physical movement into a musical rhythm. He indicates the beat, and the car slows down gently and stops not just at the right point in the road but at the end of a bar. Patiently and good-humouredly, Karajan practises this over long journeys, and he is always right: even when the traffic conditions produce surprises, his entries are always correct, he counts quietly to himself, and the car comes to a halt on the last crotchet of the bar, so to speak.

All who have flown with the conductor in the past have shown themselves fascinated by his flying skills, his colleagues go into raptures about how safe they feel when he himself is at the controls, and his interviewer, somewhat timid by nature, is prepared to believe them, without having had the experience for himself. Karajan is in a sense making music when piloting an aircraft or driving a car, so that nothing can ever go wrong. The only thing you don't notice here is the way of waiting for a transition to some new rhythm, something Karajan recalls Wilhelm Furtwängler doing. Quite the opposite, what one finds here is Herbert von Karajan's own characteristic way of determining the rhythm and bending it to suit his will. Any other way and you would not feel safe.

'It is exciting to discover just how much can be photographed. Musical motivation, for example. And how it all hangs on a fraction of a second. To give you just a single instance: at a live concert the audience sees the chorus get to their feet behind the conductor, wait for him to give them their entry and then begin to sing. And what the audience sees is simply a mass of people singing. In a film you can generate an incredible amount of tension – tension which is already present in the music, I hasten to add – if you photograph the tiny moment before a choral entry. So it's not important for a camera to know when the entry is, what it *has* to be able to show and suggest is the tension which every single singer feels before he opens his mouth. Then the actual entry comes and hits the spectator and listener like a thunderbolt.'

Once Herbert von Karajan has recorded a work according to the method just outlined, his work, so to speak, is only just beginning. Although he now has some fifteen versions at his disposal, he describes these only as the skeleton of a film. Indeed, what he does next is to take these fifteen versions and, using equipment specially installed for him, spend days on end turning them into a version which he himself still describes as a rough version into which countless additional takes will be inserted at a later date.

The musical and visual transitions will be symbolized by images either photographed at the time of the concert or filmed in sets specially built for the purpose. A further plan is then drawn up and individual musicians and groups of instruments are again drafted in and asked to mime to a tape which has now been declared definitive. Only Karajan and his cameraman know for which bars they require extra takes – they discuss it in a secret language made up of contractions which they must have invented for themselves. Karajan and his cameraman have stored both the musical and the planned visual sequence of the film, bar by bar, in their heads, and they know, in spite of the fact that they are always working on several films at once, at what point they still have to shoot this or that angle for this or that film. It is fascinating to be able to listen into these planning discussions. On top of the difficulties involved in co-ordinating all the other deadlines, there are also the deadlines of the orchestra players to be taken into account. They may have worked on the film weeks or even months previously and are now required to be available all over again.

Although the major project 'Home Video' has been handed over to an independent firm with its own enormous workforce,

one has the impression that Herbert von Karajan remains ultimately and uniquely responsible, as, indeed, he would wish to
be. Responsible, that is, according to his own interpretation of
the word, which means that he himself sees to the preparations
of even the briefest takes and has a mental record of all the plans
according to which the players are divided up and rehearsed.
In his own way he confirms as much. 'I have said so on many
occasions. I was not born to work according to somebody else's
dictates. I bide my time until I get what I want. I always wait
until it's possible to demand absolute freedom and to have that
demand met. The same is true of my films. They are intended
to demonstrate my way of making music in a form for which I
alone am responsible. In this way they are intended to survive
the passage of time and to last.'

Although Herbert von Karajan does not preface his remarks
with sentences such as these, but interjects them as though
they were self-evident, they sum up the essence of his present
work. He makes his music films in 'absolute freedom' and
entirely according to his own dictates. He founded a firm to
make them, gave it a name and hired staff, and he knows in
precisely what circumstances he intends to show these films and
at what level of interest he intends to pitch them. 'Telemondial',
with its headquarters in Monaco, is the firm that produces
Karajan's films. According to Karajan, a number of institutions
and individuals have a holding in the firm, though in actual fact
'Telemondial' is a luxury to which Karajan treats himself. 'Many
people have hobbies or interests that are expensive. I allow myself
the luxury of this firm and invest not only a financial contribution
which could be measured in terms of my fee, what I invest most
of all is the whole of my time and artistic commitment.'

There are contracts. The sound recordings are produced in
the closest co-operation with the firm with which Herbert von
Karajan has a recording contract. As far as the technical equipment and camera teams are concerned, a private firm with
headquarters in Switzerland generally makes its services available. In the case of opera recordings, there are special arrangements with television companies. The most important rule is
always that Herbert von Karajan's closest colleagues should

113

have a right to comment on all essential matters. Working with the firm in question on a private basis gives Karajan the chance to make recordings efficiently and without wasting time – Karajan always works with private industry whenever he feels it necessary to do so – while all the teams and all the equipment he needs are placed at his disposal, so that nothing can come between him and his passion.

In retrospect, Herbert von Karajan dates this decision to work for posterity to the founding of the Easter Festival. 'That was the moment I decided that from now on I was only going to do things where I myself could maintain complete control and where I wouldn't have to ask other people for their opinion.' As far as opera films are concerned, Karajan himself is saddened, of course, to think that at that time he had neither the energy nor the opportunity to begin the necessary recordings at his own expense and under his sole responsibility. At that time he was still under contract to Leo Kirch, although the two men have since drifted completely apart. His opera films, which are still owned by Kirch's firms, are, as it were, prodigal children with whom he can have nothing more to do. From the list of stage productions which were not filmed in Salzburg but which he considers worth remembering are *Boris Godunov*, *Salome* and *The Mastersingers of Nuremberg*. And he admits in all sincerity, 'I think back on these performances with immense pleasure and am filled with sadness to think that they can no longer be filmed. But it's simply too late for that now. Neither the casts nor the sets are available any longer. And I don't think I have the strength any longer to recreate them all over again. In any case, if I were to remain loyal to my own ideas, I should first have to look round again for an ideal cast and begin from scratch. It simply can't be done. I've already been saddled once with that particular burden or joy, depending on how you look at it. It's not possible to do so a second time.'

For some Salzburg productions one ought indeed to find a space in the schedule of future Festivals; the casts which Karajan himself considers ideal ought to be made available, and the agreements that are normally made with major broadcasting companies for opera performances could then be signed.

114

The broadcasting companies in question would then make the technical equipment available, negotiate the rights to a direct relay or a delayed broadcast and hand over to 'Telemondial' the material that Herbert von Karajan could then use to produce his own film version of the opera.

If Karajan now states emphatically that it is too late for all this, we may well regard this, too, as a question of time. The tapes that he has recorded to date for his opera and concert films are stored in a safe in Switzerland, while the copies on which he is currently working are stacked floor-to-ceiling on stands in the cellar next to his cutting room. And yet he remains unruffled: 'We've got the basic material here for a decent repertory. There's still a lot to record, and it may take years until I can release all the definitive versions. But I have hoarded what I've worked on, and I know that my work has not been in vain. If ever we come on the market, it won't be with the odd project but with a respectable number of programmes, offering a unity that no one else can match.'

Karajan feels confident – confident not only of his capacity for hard work, but also because he knows of no serious competition. He thinks there is no other firm and almost certainly no other colleague of his who would approach this task with his high standards, and that the quality he promises will finally be worth it.

What he has been planning, working on and perfecting in every free moment over recent years is very much his artistic testament with which he hopes to preserve his philosophy of music and to record a significant period in terms of musical interpretation. 'I know all the things that people reproach me for today, and I know that the world of music will keep on changing. That really doesn't disturb me. I have something to say and something I want to leave behind. And I know that I can only do my work alone.'

And Karajan knows that his wish to leave behind not only records but also films has nothing to do with personal vanity. 'I told you I went by bicycle to Bayreuth to see Arturo Toscanini at work. I'd have crawled to Bayreuth on my knees if I could have found a document there that would have shown me how

Hans Richter used to conduct. He was the authentic interpreter of Wagner's works, like me he was concert director of the Gesellschaft der Musikfreunde, he was an ideal conductor of the works of his beloved Johannes Brahms. The last time he conducted was in 1912. We don't know anything else about the way he conducted. We can read in any encyclopaedia that Brahms praised him for his "particular fidelity to the work", and yet we have no idea what it sounded like when Brahms called Hans Richter's interpretations of his music "faithful to the work".

'As I see it, I shall be available for coming generations to regard me as a kind of ultimate witness to our age. Just as I believe in the future of music, so I believe in the interest and curiosity of future generations. And just as I believe in the way of making music that I represent, so it seems only right to satisfy that interest for the benefit of many generations to come.'

Now in his eightieth year and watched, furthermore, by an anxious world, Herbert von Karajan withdraws into his private laboratories far more often than is realized, mixing films with the sort of respect which, in his view, should be shown to documents.

Although one can no longer speak of an experimental stage in the context of music films, there is still a long way to go before the industry reaches the level of development found in another vast area of sound reproduction, that of records, or most recently, compact discs. And, as Herbert von Karajan knows only too well and as he can demonstrate from countless anecdotes, he is one of the oldest living witnesses to the history of the gramophone record. There is no complete catalogue of all his recordings. But even the list of his recordings currently available commands more than respect, often arousing feelings more akin with envy and hatred. Is there an area of music on which Herbert von Karajan has not left his mark? Are there areas of special interest that have never attracted him? Nothing of the sort. In rather more than fifty years of making recordings Herbert von Karajan has worked with every leading orchestra and almost every leading soloist. Whatever may come of 'Home Video', Herbert von Karajan's musical development is almost fully documented on records and is so extensive that it is virtually inconceivable that a complete Karajan anthology will ever be issued.

Karajan himself describes himself as 'incredibly lucky' to have grown up with the developing medium. He has his particular opinions on modern recording techniques and interpretation, but he is also fond of recalling the infancy of the gramophone.

In fact, I can remember no more striking example of Herbert von Karajan's sense of humour than his account, now captured on tape, of what can be heard on very old recordings of Beethoven conducted by some of the performers whom Wilhelm Furtwängler admired. According to Karajan, what one hears is all manner of hissing, the odd trace of Beethoven and, finally, the fact that Franz Schalk took Beethoven very quickly. Anyone who is interested in old recordings may well be able to imagine what a revelation it is to hear Herbert von Karajan imitating scratchy needles and scarcely identifiable bits of Beethoven. The reader will, however, have to be satisfied with this brief indication, since Karajan's rendition cannot be reproduced in written form.

If Karajan remembers the recordings he made when he was still barely twenty-five, it is not only because they were made under intolerable conditions but, more especially, because he wants to refresh people's memories of the marvellous progress that has already been made in this area. 'Just imagine how we performed in those days. We played on to wax discs. There was a very simple technical device which ensured as regular as possible a running time for the disc. And every individual take was four minutes long at most. If a mistake were to creep in during those four minutes, or if the machine broke down, the whole thing had to be repeated. And repeated until all four minutes had been put on disc with all possible precision. This had an effect on the players' nerves. In other words, any mistake that was made happened not just once but every time – often until the orchestral player in question was too tired to go on playing. This alone caused difficulties which kept not only the recording technicians but above all the conductor and players in a state of constant tension. And, of course, all those comic things happened which you still hear stories about, I've experienced almost all of them myself. For example, we finally got a recording on disc after numerous attempts – all four minutes of it, completely faultless – but unfortunately we also got the grateful sigh of relief of the player who had finally managed to play the piece without a mistake. Which meant, of course, that we had to start all over again.'

With stories such as these Herbert von Karajan might almost be considered a *raconteur*. He also remembers that it was the father of one of the members of the Vienna Philharmonic who was the first radio announcer to use a four-letter word on the airwaves. He had just finished reading the late news and thought he was no longer being broadcast, but he was. He expected to be lynched, but instead he received a tremendous amount of support from radio listeners. His son, a flautist, reminded Karajan of this story in 1986, and it is one which the conductor treasures and is fond of repeating, since it is about a microphone that was switched off too late.

He has often told how, even later, when far better technical facilities were available, he had difficulty finding a few quiet minutes when recording with the Berlin Philharmonic: 'Before the Philharmonie existed and we didn't have an ideal studio, we made our recordings in Berlin in a church which lay directly beneath the approach path to Tempelhof airport. What that meant was that, although all our equipment had developed, we could still only work for three minutes without being interrupted. In other words, here, too, there were very many takes that could not be used and all the players would very quickly grow nervous, so that after a time it was simply no longer possible to go on.'

There is certainly no other conductor who has taken such an interest in every aspect of record production, including what happens to the recording after the sessions in the studio, and none who has made such widespread use of all the available technical possibilities. As a musician, however, he is interested first and foremost in recording at least a whole movement from a symphony in a single take. Quite apart from the changing fashions in the way music is recorded live from the concert hall, quite apart from the recordings that are carefully edited in the studio, and the discs whose perfection is the result of scissors and tape, Karajan is of the opinion that the ability to play well suffers if the performers are not able to record long sections in a single take. And for that one needs much more, of course, than today's technological facilities.

'When I speak of technological progress, I don't mean cassettes, or stereo, or whatever. What I remember most of all from our first recording of the Beethoven symphonies with the Berliners is how much time we had to spend on microphone tests. It took us some thirty-six hours to establish where the microphones needed to be placed. Beethoven was not an ideal composer in terms of gramophone records. What I mean is that we kept having to change the position of the orchestra players and to rearrange the microphones in order to be able to give at least an approximate idea of what Beethoven himself wanted. I told Walter Legge at the time that it would be paradise on earth for me if I could come straight into a concert hall or studio, take off my coat and start conducting. And I have lived to see this development come about. What once seemed paradise to me is now possible with proper professional firms. You arrive, you try out a few brief run-throughs, and you can then forget the microphones and concentrate on the music.' And Karajan is enough of a realist to remind his listener that this perfect state which has now been achieved has also brought down the cost of recording. The fees which a top-flight orchestra now demands and receives for a single session would make recording under the old system prohibitively expensive. The dates that are now available to make recordings would mean a considerable reduction in the number of recordings available if technology had not developed.

Karajan fairly indulges in reminiscences when talking about records. And, of course, he also remembers catastrophes. After the war, when he was recording for EMI with the Vienna Philharmonic in the Grosser Musikvereinssaal, there were insuperable difficulties in obtaining enough free dates for the orchestra. In spite of their delight at being paid guaranteed fees in foreign currency, the Philharmonic often had so many performances to give at the opera, on tour or at concerts that it was difficult to record a single symphony within the space of six weeks. But according to Karajan the orchestra was 'in a state' at that time which made it possible, once the right mood had been achieved,

119

to maintain that mood even over a period of six weeks and to make a self-contained recording. On wax discs, of course.

'Then the discs were flown to London, something I'll never forget. I went with them. The whole of the material went by a Dakota, we had to land in Frankfurt to refuel. We were still waiting on the runway when the fog came down, so we groped our way over the airfield towards the exit, and spent the night in the town. The next morning we learned that eighty per cent of the discs had frozen and cracked. The music we'd performed over several weeks, all that serious work was lost for ever.'

If Herbert von Karajan keeps on telling this tale, one understands not only what he means by wasted energy but also why he values tapes more highly than any other technological development. Pioneered during the war, this was a process which was only used at a relatively late date for sound recordings. But the day finally came when it was fully perfected and when it was also cheap enough to be used.

'Tapes freed us musicians from having to begin all over again if a single mistake were made. And they gave us musicians the chance to continue playing in spite of minimal mistakes on the way. We suddenly knew that we could again be almost carefree in our playing, and this was really the great revolution in the field of records. The relief felt by the musicians seems to me more important and greater than the fascination on the part of the technicians who, right from the outset, were enthusiastic about the idea of being able to cobble together a perfect recording from an infinite number of tiny pieces of tape. Of course, this possibility certainly exists in principle. But it's equally clear that it's only of secondary importance to a musician. There is nothing that has not been tried at least once during the history of the record industry: tenors have had their top notes spliced into place, and the most sophisticated things have been made possible by cobbling together several takes. But I find it marvellous that people were prepared to forget all that.'

For Karajan it goes without saying that in the age of the compact disc (in which he believes with fanatical zeal) a system has been rediscovered which allows music to be recorded as 'naturally' as possible, while reserving all the technological advantages for a later stage, when serious errors in the recording can be put right.

It is worth recalling at this point that Herbert von Karajan has come to terms and experimented with every innovation as soon as it has appeared. Indeed, this has sometimes even been held against him. When Hubert Bognermayr in Linz offered to use a digital sound system to devise a programme that would produce an ideal replica of the sound of the bells in Wagner's *Parsifal*, Karajan accepted the suggestion without hesitation, and when he produced the work at the Salzburg Easter Festival, he agreed to engage not only the Berlin Philharmonic but also a computer programmer.

He does not mention such things in conversation, it has always been self-evident that he would immediately accept whatever innovations were offered, as long as they were artistically justifiable. And since it *is* self-evident, he has always been in the vanguard of change. But even this he would not claim for himself, he simply says that he has devoted his life to the developing medium of gramophone records, and that he has never missed anything yet.

'When tapes came along, with all their possibilities, we musicians felt relief more than anything else. Simply because the torment of performing short takes and always having to invest them with renewed emotion resulted in extremely difficult conditions, and the fact that we could finally devote ourselves first and foremost to the music again was a marvellous feeling. The development of the long-playing gramophone record was the exact counterpart for the listener or consumer: he suddenly didn't have to keep on changing records, and could again listen to music as music.'

There was a brief phase, now almost forgotten, which Herbert von Karajan did not take seriously and which he did not become involved in. Quadrophonic sound did not seem to him to represent necessary progress in terms of the medium and it was never able, he says, to offer what is important to him, namely to give the music lover a clearer idea of what the musician is trying to express. With the compact disc, by contrast, Herbert von Karajan has been fascinated from the word go. Thanks to his friendship with the founder and first president of Sony and also with the latter's son and successor, Karajan has watched this system develop from its first beginnings and has always made himself available at public demonstrations in order to guarantee that these events would find corresponding coverage in the media. Although he has a long memory and remembers exactly how many decades ago it was claimed that records had reached their ultimate peak of perfection, he is not afraid to claim now that compact discs have finally reached a standard beyond which further developments in recording techniques are scarcely likely.

Karajan qualifies his remark, explaining in more detail what he means. 'Of course I know that technological progress is never-ending. Digital tapes have now been brought on to the market, far too soon after the introduction of compact discs, so that they may even have harmed the rapid growth of compact discs. Certainly, this rapid development has caused the industry financial harm, and it wasn't even what people call artist-friendly.'

What Karajan means is not difficult to explain. Compact discs are still far from offering music lovers all the repertory they would like to have. And the 'market' is still far from saturated, there are still plenty of music lovers who have yet to make up their minds to buy the equipment needed to play compact discs. And already something 'new' has come on to the market. There is also the danger that this new medium will devalue a particularly important quality of the slightly older medium.

Digital tapes make it possible to copy tracks from a compact disc. The digital tape can itself be copied as many times as one likes, thus giving those pirates a chance who have always been the natural enemies of the black disc and who would have been defeated by the compact disc. 'We shouldn't fool ourselves. Thanks to compact discs, it was no longer possible for amateurs to make recordings of the same technical quality or even to copy them for friends. They had neither the technical means at their disposal nor the chance to make such recordings themselves, should the means become available. And for commercial pirates unauthorized recordings or recuts would have been unprofitable.

But now ambition on the part of technicians has harmed both the industry and the artist, and also, to a certain extent, the music lover. It is now more difficult for the industry to promote one new product in the face of another. The artists, in turn, will not receive all the royalties to which they're entitled, instead they'll know that there are recordings available throughout the world for which they rehearsed and performed, but for which no one has paid the contractually agreed price. And the music lover will not only have a twinge of conscience at enjoying listening to stolen goods, he will also have recordings which have suffered a loss in quality and which are sold so cheaply that he can play them on any cheap piece of equipment – in other words, he won't hear the sort of quality that was originally invested in the recordings.

'But of course this is principally a commercial question which I do not want to discuss. I am convinced that, in the course of a long development and with the invention of the digital system, recording techniques have found what we musicians have always wanted. It is possible in principle to give the listener the tonal experience that the interpreter wanted to convey during the recording session itself and during whatever editing may then be necessary. If I had my way, the industry would now concentrate above all on developing the equipment used for playing discs, and ensure that the music lover really enjoys the same degree of tonal luxury as was achieved in the recording studio.'

With his appeal to quality as a characteristic in which Herbert von Karajan firmly believes, and with his repeated use of the key expressions 'sound' and 'luxury', Karajan has steered the conversation irresistibly round to the present and to the recordings he has made in recent years. 'I think that in recording music for records and films there has been too little concern so far for what is after all the main thing, the sound which the music lover finally hears, and the relationship of this sound to the musical experience which is offered him in the concert hall.'

For Karajan there is an enormous difference here. What the music lover hears in the concert hall is, on the one hand, live music in the very act of being created, but, on the other hand, certain details of the sound that another music lover, sitting in a different seat at the same concert, will probably not hear.

123

Moreover, Karajan thinks, at least at the time of the concert, both of them will hear a different sound from the one that the conductor himself hears. 'Naturally, I know the music first and foremost from my own position in the hall. And of course I'm capable of giving any rendition the sort of nuances that mean my tonal ideas are realized not so much for my own benefit as for the listener in the auditorium. There are enough rehearsals for that, and I'm sufficiently familiar with the acoustic properties of the spaces in which I perform. None the less, I know that even in favourable circumstances such as these it is almost impossible to convey the same impression to the audience as I myself hear, or want to hear, at the concert. In the case of gramophone recordings, by contrast, this possibility does exist, at least in theory. I can intervene in a regulatory capacity both during the recording and afterwards, and can ultimately achieve the sound which I hear in the studio and which the music lover hears who then buys the record. Even so, I have to admit that this, too, is only theoretical. Only in rare moments during my long career as an interpreter have I sensed the feeling of happiness which arises when your own ideas of a composition actually coincide with what you've produced. But these rare moments do exist, and they show what is still possible under ideal conditions. But ideal conditions mean that you work with musicians you can trust, that you have a team of colleagues who know exactly what's what, and, finally, that we are all of us able to translate our ideas into technical terms.

'Many years ago I was fortunate enough to find Michel Glotz. He and I have the same ears. I know this is so from many recordings we've made together, and it has also been confirmed by the moments of happiness of which I've spoken. He hears what I'd like to hear. What this means in practice is that it still infuriates me when he interrupts a recording and raises objections. But when I then listen to the recording at the point he interrupted me, I always know he was right. He not only hears the mistakes that I may miss while I'm conducting. He notices much more than the fact that an entry was not ideal or that my beat suddenly became too slow. These are things that any very good recording manager can hear. Michel Glotz hears

124

more. He hears where all of us – the orchestra and me – deviate from the interpretation which we are in fact aiming to achieve. This fulfils the first important requirement.'

Herbert von Karajan is fond of stating that he refuses to be told what to do by other people, and yet here he makes an astonishing exception. Not only that, he repeats the sentence, varying it slightly. 'He and I have the same ears. What he hears and the way he hears it – ultimately it's always my own version.'

For Karajan the work doesn't end where it ends for many conductors, when a so-called perfect version of the piece is on tape and everyone who has heard it agrees they are satisfied. Only now does the real work begin for Herbert von Karajan, for in his case there is never only one perfect version but several apparently wholly successful recordings, from which the final takes are chosen and edited together. Here, too, it is Michel Glotz who makes the choice in reality. In their long years of work together, he has acquired the right to make the choice on his own. None the less, Karajan generally insists on listening in, even if only to acknowledge that his colleague is right. And he knows, too, that he is more or less alone in his oft-quoted love of perfection. 'I know that very many of my younger colleagues no longer have time for the work that is done after the recording session is over, that they leave the acoustic control and editing of the tapes to the experts at the firm in question, sometimes they even decline to check the end result. Things are made relatively easy for them, and they make things somewhat too easy for themselves. I belong to another age. I have a different conception of the conductor's job. I alone am responsible for the recording, which means that I also have to consider the ultimate sound of the recording, which is not achieved with the orchestra but at the mixing desk. This is something on which there are different opinions, but one on which I have always expressed a firm view. Anyone who buys a record or compact disc always hears something that is different from, or more than, what the orchestra played in the studio under its conductor. He hears a recording. And so I must also take an interest in this recording and ultimately ensure that it coincides with my own view of music.'

Karajan's Beautiful Sound

What Karajan had to say on this subject was said not just once but many times, and in various ways, in the course of our recorded conversations. It goes back to what he described in his conversations about visual presentation as his one major concern. It is the question of interpretation.

'Whenever people say that I am always striving to achieve a beautiful sound, I agree with them, and take it not as a reproach but as a compliment for something I work hard to produce. If people say that I smooth out the corners, my reply is that I believe that in music there is nothing to smooth out. The orchestral sound that people associate with me or which they describe in apparently critical terms arises entirely of its own accord. I ask the orchestra to hold on to every note that the composer has written, sustaining it for its full length and not allowing it to grow weaker before the end of note value indicated in the score. The result, of course, is a somewhat different tonal impression from the one you'll hear in many other recordings. But I stand by this. Perhaps it's old-fashioned. Maybe there'll be a different development in the future, one that is equally correct or explicable. I don't know of it, I have never heard it anywhere. What I hear on those occasions when people perform in a way that differs expressly from the one I have learned to follow throughout my life is no more than a fashion, I feel, a so-called trend.

'Let me explain what I mean. What I understand by a fashionable trend is people's fondness for speaking of "Mozart today". Even the expression I consider presumptuous. And I find little sense in what people declare to be new today. If they remind me, for instance, of the forces with which Mozart performed and recommend me to use original instruments from Mozart's time, I couldn't be more content. We all know how skilful Mozart was at adapting his writing to suit prevailing circumstances and above all how happy he was if a larger body of strings was placed at his disposal. And as for original instruments, my ears are too sensitive not to notice that they are not even able to remain in tune today. With most of the "original" performances that I'm familiar with, musicians who can normally tune their instruments with relative precision suddenly sound very impure when playing together. No one can claim that this is inaudible – and no one, I hope, will claim that Mozart wrote intentionally for poorly tuned groups of instruments. And as for the sound of original instruments, they sound scratchy. The fascination that stems from this sound is something I've never felt for myself.'

There is something both self-conscious and at the same time modest about the somewhat different picture that Karajan projects of himself in this context. 'Of course I'm biased on all questions of interpretation. Of course people can say that, as a musician, I'm stuck in a rut. Of course it is inevitable that after all the decades during which I have been making music and achieving what I want, I should have a firm standpoint, which I can defend. And of course I do not presume to judge the future. It will come and bring changes and will in turn displace a sound which exists today as a mere fashion, together with all its interpreters – but even before that stage is reached, all today's interpreters will have changed, since art, like life, involves permanent change.'

Once he has warmed to a subject, Karajan becomes highly pugnacious and keen to discuss, but what he reveals most of all is that he knows very well the opinion that people have of him.

'Many of my critics write, and will go on writing, that I conduct too lavishly. That may be so. During my day people have been somewhat extravagant in terms of art and music. I believed this was the right attitude to adopt, and so I've supported it. It has something to do with respect towards art, and if this respect is old-fashioned, so be it, I've no intention of dissociating myself from it. When I was young, we approached music with a sense of awe and celebrated each such approach as a special event. I can

128

see, of course, that times have changed, that people don't want to know about respect any longer, and that it is not in keeping with the times to celebrate a concert. People are going to great lengths to make themselves ugly, to wear ugly clothes, and to feel precious little enthusiasm for beauty. I've been observing this for years, I've even noticed it in my daughters, who consciously go around looking as unkempt as possible, since that's the fashion. I know there's nothing that can be done at present to change all this. But no one can expect me to seek a polite or understanding explanation for this, still less that I should agree with it and conform. I belong to a different age. And what I want to preserve for myself and posterity also belongs to a different age.

'My so-called beautiful sound is something, furthermore, that I'm convinced by. As all the orchestra players with whom I've worked in recent years will confirm, it is basically a reaction against what I've elsewhere described as falsifying documents. Just as, in the case of stage productions, I do not understand or appreciate why producers ignore the author's own instructions, or why they try to make the audience ignore them in favour of their own original ideas, what concerns me at concert rehearsals is simply as correct a rendition of the notes as possible. You can prove this for yourself, because if you think back over the decades, you'll be able to confirm that I've got by at rehearsals with having to say only a very few sentences. I don't know how often I've said them, but I do know that I still say them at all my rehearsals with the Philharmonic orchestras in Berlin and Vienna and that I have to repeat them particularly often if I've not performed with one or the other orchestra for a certain period of time. Every good orchestra has certain characteristics, and my two outstanding orchestras naturally differ from each other. Even so, there is one sentence which I have to say to each orchestra – repeatedly during rehearsals – "Gentlemen, what you're playing is simply not true".'

Karajan explains what he means by singing out loud with great enthusiasm. He explains how he wants something played by starting to conduct, even when there is only one other person in the room. Ultimately one realizes that his explanations would need to be shown on film to be properly convincing.

He argues, for example, that orchestral players have a habit of constantly interrupting their playing. They play note by note, not one of which is held to the very end, in other words, to the point at which the note that follows comes into its own. To quote Karajan's favourite example: every orchestra thinks that a chord which has to be played *forte*, that is, loudly, must start *forte* but that, since the intensity naturally dies away, the sound can also fade away slowly. 'The last time we performed Anton Bruckner's *Te Deum*, I spent a great deal of time and a good deal of effort ensuring that the final chord ended as powerfully as it began. I managed to do it. The final chord stood there like a monument. I'll never forget it.'

For the conductor Herbert von Karajan it appears that the problems of musical interpretation can always be reduced to these 'few sentences' and others like them, and to insights which leave a lay person feeling bewildered. To take the example of so-called tricky passages in a score. Karajan sees these passages as ones where not every player knows exactly what relation his own part bears to that of his colleagues. There are brass chords in Richard Strauss which, according to Karajan, can never be played absolutely cleanly and which were obviously never intended to sound absolutely pure. And there are many more superficial problems which emerge in the course of decades as a result of orchestras always performing from their own material, a practice which leads to tempo variations. In order to save space or to locate a page turn at a more convenient point, a note engraver may have compressed bars together and thus misled generations of players into altering the tempo, a change which is solely the result of the optical impression made by the notes and has nothing to do with the composer's intentions.

When Herbert von Karajan speaks of falsifying documents, he is never at a loss for all manner of examples. He remembers a producer who, for visual reasons, would have nothing to do with the shattered fragments of the sword Nothung in the final act of *The Valkyrie*. He is reminded of the most recent successful productions of Mozart's operas, including a *Magic Flute* which he no longer recognized, although he could hear very clearly how badly it was sung. But immediately afterwards he grows more accommodating and recalls Victor De Sabata whose memory of orchestral scores was second to none and who suffered perpetually from hearing wrongly played notes – documentary falsification which cannot be stamped out.

As for those scores mentioned above which have led whole generations of orchestra players to read false tempi into them, Karajan would certainly not accept the simplest of all remedies, namely, to have new and better editions printed. He is, after all, a pragmatist and knows that orchestral players write in their parts, and that these notes in turn become a part of music history, an eloquent commentary on the life of the orchestra. 'After all, they perform from this material throughout their entire lives, it becomes a part of them, you can't take it away from them. Their eyes have grown used to it – orchestral players, after all, only ever look at their music, almost never at the conductor. Only the leader forms an exception here, he plays by heart and gives the conductor the particular pleasure of showing an interest in him . . .'

As a pragmatist he readily admits that much has changed in the course of the decades he has been conducting. The players' technical capabilities have improved enormously, the precision of their playing has increased perceptibly, the repertoire has grown in size, and the ability to read a new piece quickly and accurately has also become much greater. Certain habits of course can still not be permanently eradicated, but if they have to be drummed out of the players on each new occasion, then Karajan sees it as the duty of a conductor of his stature to do so. After all, he belongs to another age.

He is given scarcely any more time than a younger colleague would be given to recover from one exhausting concert tour and prepare for an important series of recordings. But Karajan doesn't need time to do so. He confers with his colleagues and uses the interval to announce the final programme for the 1988 Easter Festival. He will produce and conduct *Tosca*. His audience, which comes to the Easter Festival largely because of him, will have no reason on this occasion to complain, however discreetly, that they are seeing a production they have seen before. They will have something new.

And his closest colleagues, to whom outsiders often turn to verify rumours or half-formed sentences muttered by the maestro at open rehearsals, remain silent, although they know very well that Herbert von Karajan's plans extend far beyond 1988. Not only does he intend to be available to serve on the 1991 Salzburg Festival committee and to 'direct' *Don Giovanni*, he is also making his own private plans at least up until that time, and is certainly not thinking of giving up the Easter Festival before he has to.

The subject has already come up many times in conversation. Now that there are close links between the two major festivals in Salzburg (both of which are enormously overbooked), and now that the production costs are shared on an equitable and necessary basis, he is prepared to think aloud about the future of the Easter Festival. 'Of course it'll continue, even after I've stopped conducting. There's no question of that. It has proved itself in the town, it's got its own audience, it has its own slot in the Salzburg calendar. I've no illusions about it, but I've no worries either. The people in Salzburg who are responsible for it certainly won't think of allowing something like the Easter Festival to pass away. They'd be stupid not to keep on with an institution which attracts so much attention and brings so much money to the town.' And once again the attentive listener thinks how much more instructive it would be to have a video of the conversation rather than a résumé or literal account. For Herbert von Karajan, normally tired and clearly in pain, becomes almost amusing when he imagines the future of a festival which he founded more than two decades ago and which he has run with an iron resolve exclusively according to his own ideas.

'I know exactly how it will be. As soon as we announce the two opera performances for the Easter Festival and the tickets go on sale, we could sell at least thirty times as many tickets. When I'm no longer there to conduct, things may change. It may be that demand for tickets will fall off initially and that they'll be only ten times oversubscribed. However, there'll still be more than enough opera lovers wanting to come to the Easter Festival. And I'll no longer be there and no longer have to worry about it.' And, no doubt knowing that we would all like to hear something about the conductor whom he wants to take over the running of the Festival, Herbert von Karajan, far from falling silent, adopts a jocular tone. 'Do you know what it will be like? There'll be exactly the same intrigues that there have always been in Salzburg and everywhere else for that matter.'

He has no great wish to speak on the subject, but above all he does not wish to be misunderstood. He simply wants to suggest that he has got to know the world, and especially his own world, and that he has long since rid himself of any illusions. Even if he regards himself as the last representative of a certain period in European music-making and devotes his energies to capturing that period in music and images in order to hand them on to the next generation, he none the less knows that there is nothing final about it. Things will go on, he says. And he is certainly not saddened or appalled at this state of affairs. For the record, he prefers it to be known that it would rather amuse him to see all the efforts which will be undertaken by various individuals and institutions to lay hands on something that is currently more than safe in his own hands.

And he remains unwilling to give advice to those who may already secretly be thinking about who will take over which of his present functions. Why should he? As he himself sees the situation, he is artistic director for life of the Berlin Philharmonic and has to get on with his players, providing a sense of continuity and ensuring that what is now the youngest generation also bears his stamp. 'Our work together has lasted for generations. While it has certainly borne fruit, it is now increasingly a mental burden to me. Time and again I arrive at a rehearsal and am told that another player is leaving, another member of the Berlin Philharmonic is retiring. It comes as a shock on each new occasion, and I'm almost at a loss to know what I should say at such a moment. Do you intend to leave me completely alone? That's what I ask them, more or less. But at the same time I know that since the beginning of our so-called marriage there have always been new members coming along and that they will pass on what we have achieved together.'

Karajan says no more on the subject, he has had unfortunate experiences in the past through mentioning names. Whenever he has spoken publicly about a colleague and made expressly positive or even polite references to other conductors, people have interpreted his remarks as a reference to his successor's identity, in spite of the apparent absurdity of such assumptions. When, for example, he stressed his high regard for the Italian maestro Carlo Maria Giulini, almost everybody ignored Giulini's age and declared that Karajan had recommended him as the next director of the Berlin Philharmonic. That is presumably why Karajan is now so sparing in his public pronouncements and why, even in private conversation, he rarely names conductors he thinks highly of. He does not want to be misunderstood, he does not want to hurt anyone, but nor, indeed, has he any intention of handing over to a successor.

On the other hand, one sometimes hears it said by members of his entourage that he is not afraid of speaking openly about the fact that he will not conduct, make music and live for ever. Sometimes he even takes pleasure in frightening those people who dare not discuss the matter in his presence by referring to what they have often thought about in private. Even so, Herbert von Karajan really won't commit himself. He sprinkles his conversation with remarks such as 'And when I die, all the out-of-focus photographs of me will be published', and at the same time watches whoever he happens to be talking to very closely.

At the same time, however, he is making plans years ahead and has organized his life in such a way as to be able to realize the majority of them. To the outside observer at least it seems inconceivable that Herbert von Karajan will ever retire. He once gave the impression of wanting to survive as a radiant athletic hero and was even prepared to put up with a number of operations and a great deal of pain to achieve that ideal. He has since thought better of it. He has accepted the pain and the illness which has reduced his activities, and has attempted to make something even of them.

'Of course, my reduced mobility is something that has brought a new period in my life: I can acquire music all over again. I never take a pessimistic view of my life, even now I have recognized the advantages and turned them to good account. As a result of this more or less enforced rest I've time to study music and listen to it again. And even time to listen to all my recordings again. In doing so I sense where my own inner harmony with the music was disturbed – and I think of ways to restore it, and wish I could record it all again. I now know better than I did then how music must sound. I've time now to see this for myself, quietly and calmly, time to establish this for myself. I'm bound to see it as a kind of blessing that my physical condition forces me to be highly critical about all that I once did, at a time when there was no time for so much reflection.'

The question which follows on from this – which of his innumerable records he still treasures, which he rejects and which he might like to rerecord – he leaves unanswered. But he gives at least a hint that a number of recordings of works that are still regarded as 'popular' pieces continue to be particularly dear to his heart. He mentions his recordings from Offenbach's opera *The Tales of Hoffmann* with the Berlin Philharmonic, a piece which enchants him: he hums the Barcarole, but he also insists that the audience should be aware that what this opera is about, for all its beguiling music, is a man's death. 'There's not a single bar that's thoughtlessly written,' he says, and in a single sentence sketches a picture of Offenbach that is closer to the truth than the image that is often projected in musical circles. And in order not to exclude the Vienna Philharmonic from this more than cursory survey (not least because Herbert von Karajan's recent work with this orchestra has been marked by a hitherto unprecedented degree of trust and intimacy), he names two recordings produced with them in quick succession. He performed the Mozart *Requiem* with the orchestra and immediately afterwards made the first recordings for the only New Year's Day concert which he has ever conducted with them in the course of his entire career. He felt equally at home with the music of Mozart and Johann Strauss as he did with the players in question. He says nothing about the Mozart, since it no longer seems necessary for him to do so, but he wants his readers to know how wonderful he finds the music of Johann Strauss, music which has accompanied him throughout his entire life.

Johann Strauss's music throughout a lifetime as long as Karajan's? As in every other case, the conductor does not

135

quote examples himself, but is happy to be reminded of them. He heard Johann Strauss in his childhood days, when there were still musicians performing who had known the composer and his tempi. In Ulm he was under contract for eight years to an ensemble which had no choice but to perform Strauss's operettas as a regular part of its repertory. In his capacity as artistic director of the Vienna State Opera, he conducted a production of *Die Fledermaus*, a recording of which continues to this day to be in considerable demand. He has also recorded Strauss's music with the Berliners. But above all was his wish to conduct the 1987 New Year's Day concert, a wish he devoted a lot of energy to realizing. He not only collaborated on drawing up the programme, he also thought extensively about how best to direct the traditional television broadcast, suggesting outstanding choreographers and convincing those responsible of the need to include a sequence from the Spanish Riding School in the programme. 'I was sent a film of the Lippizaners and was enchanted by the music of Johann Strauss the Father. What particularly pleased me was being told that the music and tempo of the film were the ones that the horses were used to. I found it just right and stuck to the same tempo that the horses are used to at the Riding School.' When, shortly before the New Year's Day concert was due to take place, newspaper reports raised doubts as to his ability to appear, he himself was the first to dismiss them.

He arrived at the first rehearsals on time and well prepared, he put up with the various procedures involved in prerecording the programme for television, he conducted the traditional official final rehearsal for the Austrian Army and the 1986 New Year's Eve concert, and at the 1987 New Year's Day concert he was so alert and good-humoured that even the most attentive and allegedly most severe critics were finally at a loss for superlatives. Karajan himself was satisfied and happy from the moment he had first decided to conduct the concert. 'From the first bar onwards the orchestra and I were a single heart and soul,' he said, and for the first time in all his years of conversation as an Austrian he sounded almost Viennese. 'What can I say about Johann Strauss. He's in our blood.

136

There's really nothing that us musicians need to say on the subject.'

Nor does Karajan have anything to say about the works he still wants to record. He himself has a plan but he is not prepared to make it known in detail. It would probably not be possible to do so in any case. For he readily admits that he is so preoccupied with renewing his existing repertory that he would even remake some of the 'Home Video' recordings that he has already completed, were an opportunity to present itself. However many more years he will be able to work, his workload will continue to grow.

And he still has nothing to say about his private life, which, in spite of almost desperate entreaties, remains cut off from public inquisitiveness. His family belongs to him and certainly not to the media, at least if he has *his* way. He sees his closest colleagues as a shield and does everything to make them feel how grateful he is to them for taking on this function. His singers and players have their own stories to tell, and certainly do not expect him to do so for them. The fact that he has helped generations of singers to achieve fame and fortune is something he will not discuss. Nor does he talk about the fact that he has had to part company with many of them in the course of his career. He refuses even to be asked whether he mourns the passing of a legendary Mozart ensemble. Why will music lovers not simply accept that time does not stand still, that new singers must be found and that constant change is necessary not only in the orchestra but also on stage? Herbert von Karajan has always been particularly attracted towards relatively young interpreters and to those at the very beginning of their careers. As for those who are approaching retirement age or who are already retired, he has nothing to say.

He pays no attention to barriers of any description, including those which arise, for example, from membership of a particular race. Among the singers who have won prizes at his competitions are ones from the Soviet Union, and when he auditions singers for his Easter Festival, he invites the ones whose voices appear to him to be interesting.

At an audition for tenors to replace José Carreras in *Don Carlos*,

137

for example, a very young and particularly dark-skinned black singer stepped on to the stage, much to the astonishment of everyone present. The lighting technicians and those who were preparing for a television recording of the work groaned audibly and declared that not even with the most modern techniques would it be possible to transform the tenor into a European Don Carlos. Herbert von Karajan simply turned on them with the question, 'And what if he has the best voice?' And he worked with the promising tenor with a seriousness and intensity that made it clear no one was going to be treated differently from anyone else.

Herbert von Karajan was not prepared to offer a résumé of his life. Even his imminent eightieth birthday is a date which is more likely to be merely tiring than a decisive watershed in his career. He divides up his life somewhat differently, referring to the whole of his life up until the early 1940s as a hard school which he had to go through. After that, he says, he entered a period of enforced rest and self-reflection, while the period which followed was one of hard but successful work, a period that encompassed all his globe-trotting exploits and extended at least as far as the end of his appointment as artistic director of the Vienna State Opera. The period of his artistic maturity he dates more or less from his founding of the Easter Festival, while recent years – although he himself does not express it quite so clearly – have been a time to survey the past, a time to look in detail at his testament as an artist.

Bound up with this most recent period are the hours spent with his colleagues on the Festival committee agonizing over the future of the Salzburg Festival. He knows that the Festival may easily change when he is no longer the main attraction. He can imagine that some of the things he describes as 'falsification of documents' might gain ground in Salzburg, even if only as a fashionable trend under a much more positive name. He is enough of a realist not to worry about that sort of thing. After three generations he knows that while the Salzburg Festival appears to have a lot to offer, it in fact reflects the plans of a handful of artistic figures. Not even in the future does he believe this will change. And predictions as to who his successor may be are not to be expected from Herbert von Karajan. There is immense curiosity about who is currently attending Karajan's rehearsals in Salzburg and which conductors have been invited, apparently at his recommendation. Although no slouch in such matters, I can do more than state in black and white that Herbert von Karajan never once mentioned anyone by name. He is in contact with far more colleagues than the general public knows or discovers. He has not spoken with any of them on matters such as the question of his succession or the transition to a new era. He does not speak to anyone about things that he himself is no longer in a position to organize.

And, of course, he speaks only with extreme self-discipline and discretion about the state of his health. 'It placed a great strain on me when my illness excluded me from virtually every type of sport. I had been very active all my life and, as I now know, I put so much into sport above all that the physical repercussions are doubly serious. It hurts a lot not to be able to go skiing any more, to have to give up my yacht and not to be able to go walking in the mountains. And it has meant a decisive change in my life, not being able to go walking for hours on end as I was used to doing at all hours of the day and night. All I can do now is go swimming every day. The various operations I've had, and the infections which I've caught on various occasions recently have forced me to live an indoor life. I sit and study my scores and work on my films. I see it as a prescribed break in my life; I see myself forced to find a meaning to it, and I'm trying to see that meaning in renewed study.'

Karajan puts up with pain and afflictions calmly and concentratedly, and has no thought of presenting the general public with a pitiful picture of himself. And he has no intention of saying anything further about his private preoccupations. 'I'd have time now for almost anything – but I find it very difficult to write, and so I'm not working on my book. And as for reading, novels have never interested me. I always need to have books around me which can teach me things. In other words, I devour technical journals, keep abreast of progress and am now interested in history again. But I much prefer studying Egon Friedell. I knew him and admired him in my early days in Salzburg as a member of Max Reinhardt's entourage. I remember him not only as an amusing and witty entertainer during those famous long nights at Schloss Leopoldskron – whenever Reinhardt asked him, he would read aloud from his writings, and we would sit up half the night utterly fascinated. Even then I was impressed by the way he interpreted history and described it. I have gained an awful lot from reading his history of art, and admire the incredible fund of knowledge which he has but which he doesn't let the reader feel. I wouldn't like people to forget that what I have always admired, and what I continue to admire, are people who are real experts in their particular field – as a rule it's artistic people who always find common ground when talking to me.'

Herbert von Karajan knows that not only his admirers but the public in general have always wanted to know more about his private life, and that they have always suffered from not knowing. He has maintained a strict silence in the face of all apparently indiscreet but largely unauthorized accounts of his life, and not even deigned to issue public denials.

'The family is very important to me. I've a reputation for being unsociable. But I think that, as a characterization, it's wide of the mark. I have no time for parties, no interest in superficial conversations, no enthusiasm for receptions and such like. What I need in terms of human contact I have sought and found first and foremost with my family.

'People are mistaken when they claim that I have no time. The impression may arise because I have little time for useless conversations. Because I send my apologies whenever it's a question of appearing at public functions. The truth of the matter is that I have a great deal of time, especially now, because my illness makes it impossible for me to walk very far.

'As people probably know, I'm someone with a great sense of discipline. What that means is that throughout my life I've been used to living a very concentrated life with each day properly divided up. It's also meant that I've always had a lot of time for my family. When my children were small, I always tried to spend time with them at our house in St Moritz. We also began by sending them to school there, in order to be with them as much as possible. And it still makes me happy to think of the close contact we had at that time. We did sport together, we played together, it was a very happy time for me.

'Now that my daughters have grown up, our contact has necessarily changed.

'For my elder daughter there was basically never any question of her following any other course than the one she is now embarked on in going into the theatre. She has shown remarkable single-mindedness. She played in amateur companies, she has experimented with producing, and she's worked seriously on herself. And I'm very happy that she's now with George Tabori in Vienna, where I'm told that she's been very successful. It doesn't surprise me that she's making a career for herself, she's well-read and – like the rest of the family – she has her own tastes in music, and she knows exactly what she wants. We see each other, I know all that she gets up to, and I'm very happy to believe the good reviews she's had in Vienna. She's got talent.

'Our younger daughter spent three years living in America, she did a course in photography and is now going to go back to America to study music in Boston. She's always been very interested in music, she knows a lot, and she also knows all about an area that I really don't understand at all: she knows about pop music and rock, one of the reasons for her enthusiasm being that she can also take an active part in this sort of music.'

When Karajan speaks of his family, he is either officially reserved or, as in this case, a refreshingly proud father who admits that he is fond of his children and thinks with them, as any father must.

'My wife is completely different. Even before we met she had a real love of music and is still an enthusiastic music lover who can listen, intensively and knowledgeably, for hours on end. Her positive interest in my work has always meant a lot to me and given me additional security.

'She began to take an interest in painting at a very early age, she has a real understanding for art, and of course she has had the relevant training. She attended courses in London, for several summers she was at the Schule des Sehens in Salzburg, and she's had some good teachers.

'I'm always trying to interpret her. I never think in visual

141

terms. For me it's impossible to think in images with a piece of music; I'm convinced that even so-called programme music and works with a title added to them that is intended to evoke certain images are nothing but pure music. With *La Mer* I've never thought of the sea, I'd go further and say that I don't believe it was ever Beethoven's intention to set the countryside to music. Not even the Pastoral Symphony suggests images to me, it's just pure music to me. And the number of works for which composers have simply added a title to help their music gain popularity is by no means small.

'When I hear music or interpret it, I always want to get to its roots, and it really is nothing but pure music that I find there. In my own opinion, the same is true of my wife and her painting. In actual fact she's interested only in the roots of painting, in other words, in colours. In the demonic nature of colours. She's not a landscape painter, in her paintings she tries to express what she feels. That is more deeply thought, more important.

'Years ago she was asked to provide twenty-five paintings – they were used for a series of sleeve illustrations for some long-playing records I'd made, and the positive response to her paintings was enormous. There's now going to be another series of recordings, and, as before, my wife has been asked to provide the illustrations. She, too, has matured, so that what she paints now actually corresponds much more closely with my own frame of mind.

'Perhaps we see too few people. But I don't think that's true. Of course, my wife sometimes likes going out with friends. And of course I appear too isolated. But both she and I have a love of nature in our blood, and when we used to go walking together, that was the most important thing for us both.'

While reading through the final version of this book, Herbert von Karajan commented on some of his own remarks and on other people's reactions to the state of his health. The fact that he has lived with pain for several years now, that he subjugates his body to his will, leads him to make a remark which leaves even someone motivated by mere idle curiosity (still less an interpreter) deeply shaken: 'Whatever else may be worked into my obituary, the words on my tombstone ought to read, "After a long and painful illness . . .".'

And his closeness to Eliette von Karajan he describes in a roundabout way: 'I now take far more time to prepare for an artistic undertaking. When the Philharmonic, for example, asked me if I'd like to conduct the New Year's Day concert, I was delighted to accept the invitation. After all, the programme consists of waltzes and polkas of a kind that people like us grew up with and that we have in our blood. But then I spent three weeks thinking about nothing but the music that we were going to play. What is it really about, I wanted to know and thought about nothing but the waltzes and polkas of Johann Strauss Father and Son. And by the end I'd forgotten how this music went, I literally had it under my skin. And at the first rehearsal I conducted this music – which I had already conducted countless times before – in a completely different way. And after the concert my wife said to me, quite spontaneously, "You've become a completely different person". She understood me perfectly.'

The Foundation which bears his name and which was established in his honour by the Gesellschaft der Musikfreunde in Vienna was not just a gratefully accepted present on the occasion on his seventy-fifth birthday but a platform on which he found an opportunity to confer with the experts whom he has already mentioned. He made himself available for the Foundation's deliberations; and he almost always found time to attend the public conferences which the Foundation organized in Salzburg and Vienna. He is of the view that it is more than welcome if academics at universities and institutions are stimulated in their own way into researching music and its influence on the individual. 'All the work that has been done so far at the instigation of the Foundation has been of great interest to me. But the most important thing I gained was to get to know a number of outstanding academics from whom I have been able to learn something. And it was, of course, a source of great satisfaction to me that some of them are very gifted musicians and that, as practising musicians, too, they know something about my subject.' None the less, Herbert von Karajan concedes, when questioned more closely on the matter, that the

143

life-long experience produced by direct involvement in music is more important to him and to every musician than any scientific findings. He sees music not as an inexplicable mystery, but nor, ultimately, as an art that can be totally dissected. 'A life without music is inconceivable to me,' he says in this context and in that way defines what music means to him. It provides a meaning to life and an elixir, and, at the same time, is something that, to the sorrow of many music lovers, he almost never talks about.

That is why his library contains many books sent to him by musicologists and critics and (a source of some amusement to many an observer) including dedications that are often in crass contrast to the publicly stated views of those same critics. But that is also why he refuses to engage in almost every musicological discussion, having as low an opinion of popular 'interpreters' as he has of the authors of certain passionately written treatises. And that is why he sticks closely to the composer's own intentions, while never admitting that the study of original manuscripts is particularly close to his heart. On the one hand this kind of study contradicts his view that a work does not begin to live until it is in an interpreter's creative hands, while, on the other hand, his by no means negligible knowledge of the history of music suggests that source studies are not so important. Karajan knows very well that all composers whose original editions are now available in published form and whose autograph manuscripts are now taken so seriously, were happy in their own day to put up with all manner of alterations if such changes were necessary to ensure a performance. He knows very well what he is thinking and talking about. He knows how quickly Anton Bruckner fell in with the friendly dictates of those conductors who wanted to perform his symphonies, and he knows, too, that Wolfgang Amadeus Mozart reported gleefully each time he found a larger ensemble at his disposal than the one available in Vienna. 'We can all read about this sort of thing in books. And in Vienna enough stories have survived about Anton Bruckner to remind us that he was a man who seemed to suffer very much from his particular kind of sexuality, and who agreed to, or wrote, so many different versions of his symphonies because he never had the courage to make up his mind. Whenever people suggested a cut or wanted to change something, he bowed and gave his consent.' However committed an advocate of Bruckner's works Herbert von Karajan may be, one senses very clearly in conversation that he would prefer to describe Bruckner's much vaunted humility as a weakness on the composer's part. He has little time for weak individuals.

Although frequently recorded, Herbert von Karajan's life has only ever been revealed by him in episodic fashion. It is now a battle against illness and requires heroic effort on his part. Is Herbert von Karajan happy? The conductor simply ignores the question. Is he optimistic? This question, too, was of no interest to him. In all the recorded statements about himself there are only two which he volunteered about his life. He regards it as a meaningful life, so meaningful in fact that even all the blows of fate that he has suffered are interpreted as necessary. And he says, 'A life without making music is inconceivable to me.'

A few dates relating to Herbert von Karajan and the Vienna State Opera

Karl Böhm resigned as director of the Vienna State Opera on 5 March 1956. The company had moved back into its home on the Ringstrasse on 5 November 1955.

There were immediate reports in the press that negotiations had already begun with Herbert von Karajan as the new director.

On 13 June 1956 La Scala, Milan, gave a guest performance of *Lucia di Lammermoor* at the State Opera, with Maria Callas in the title role. The production was staged and conducted by Herbert von Karajan.

On 14 June 1956 Herbert von Karajan signed a contract appointing him artistic director of the Vienna State Opera with effect from 1 January 1957.

Herbert von Karajan's first conducting engagement in his new capacity at the Opera was on 16 January 1957 when he conducted Mozart's *Masonic Funeral Music* in memory of Arturo Toscanini.

On 2 April 1957 Karajan presented Wagner's *The Valkyrie*, his first new staging as producer and conductor.

His general secretaries were Egon Seefehlner, who went to the Deutsche Oper, Berlin, in 1961, and then Albert Moser.

Karajan resigned in February 1962, but when the rest of the opera house staff came out in sympathy, a solution was found to persuade him to withdraw his resignation. By March the people of Vienna were able to welcome him back to the city, and negotiations began with the Stuttgart intendant Walter Erich Schäfer with the aim of appointing a new co-director. Schäfer left in June 1963 and Egon Hilbert was appointed the new director. According to a memorandum drawn up at the time, Herbert von Karajan was now artistic director and director of the Vienna State Opera, while Egon Hilbert was director of the Vienna State Opera.

At the end of the 1963/64 season Karajan withdrew from his appointment as artistic director and director of the Vienna State Opera.

A few facts relating to the Salzburg Festival

In 1946 the operas *Don Giovanni, Der Rosenkavalier* and *The Marriage of Figaro* were performed in Salzburg. Herbert von Karajan was involved in the rehearsals, but was not allowed to conduct public performances. The conductors were Josef Krips, Hans Swarowsky and Felix Prohaska.

In 1947 Wilhelm Furtwängler again conducted two concerts with the Vienna Philharmonic, while Herbert von Karajan 'marked time', as he says in his autobiography.

In 1948 Wilhelm Furtwängler conducted his first opera at the post-war Festival, Beethoven's *Fidelio*. Herbert von Karajan conducted Gluck's *Orfeo* in the Felsenreitschule, *The Marriage of Figaro* in the Festspielhaus, and two orchestral concerts.

The 1949 Festival was dominated by Wilhelm Furtwängler with two operatic productions and one concert, while Herbert von Karajan conducted a performance of the Verdi *Requiem* and a concert including Beethoven's Choral Symphony. For two concerts Bruno Walter returned to Salzburg. Between 1950 and 1956 Herbert von Karajan did not conduct at all in Salzburg.

In 1957 Herbert von Karajan presented *Fidelio* in the Felsenreitschule and *Falstaff* in the Festspielhaus, both conducting and producing. He also conducted two concerts with the Vienna Philharmonic and two with the Berlin Philharmonic. A further concert with the Berlin Philharmonic was given in the Mozarteum in the framework of a series of 'Concerts of Contemporary Music' and included works by Theodor Berger, Gottfried von Einem and Arthur Honegger.

In 1958 Herbert von Karajan conducted *Don Carlos* and *Fidelio* in the Felsenreitschule, where he also led a performance of the Verdi *Requiem* with the Vienna Philharmonic.

In 1959 Herbert von Karajan conducted Gluck's *Orfeo* in the Felsenreitschule, together with a performance of Beethoven's *Missa Solemnis* with the Vienna Philharmonic.

In 1960 Herbert von Karajan conducted the official opening ceremony in the New Festspielhaus, including a performance of *Der Rosenkavalier*. He also conducted *Don Giovanni* in the Old

Festspielhaus and one concert each with the Vienna and Berlin Philharmonic Orchestras.

Since 1960 Herbert von Karajan's conducting commitments to the Salzburg Festival have been as intensive as they have been uninterrupted.

Karajan was appointed artistic director of the Festival prior to the opening of the 1956 season. He was already responsible for the 1957 programme, as he was for what is now the traditional invitation to a second international orchestra to play at the Festival.

In 1960 Herbert von Karajan's contract was declared to be 'fulfilled and ended' with the opening of the New Festspielhaus. That same year, the President of the Festival, Heinrich Puthon, retired from office and was succeeded by Bernhard Paumgartner.

In 1964 Herbert von Karajan finally resigned as artistic director of the Vienna State Opera. He was elected to serve on the Salzburg Festival committee of management during the 1964 summer Festival. He has remained on the committee ever since.